This is a call.

THE RELATIONSHIP STATUS

First Edition
Printing: December 2021

Book Cover Artist: Grace Waldner

ISBN: 978-0-645-38300-3

Sarah McCutcheon
PO Box 154
Mayfield NSW 2304
Australia

For more information about this book, you can check out

www.therelationshipstatusbook.com

gdaysarah@gmail.com

A call to rethink how we view the unmarried life in the church today.

Endorsements

Sarah takes us from the shallow waters of relationships and identity as tradition and popular culture often accepts them to be, into the depth and breadth, variety and possibilities of what the creator of human personalities wants for us. We can all identify with parts of her very personal story. Her life in community, serving the needs of people, effective communication of values and principles, strong leadership and commitment to calling, provide authority to share these things.

Dean Sherman
Author of Love, Sex and Relationships

For a subject fraught with unexamined myths, cultural and religious taboos, and plenty of unspoken pressure and rules, Sarah McCutcheon cuts through with refreshing honesty, practicality, and a grounded theology. Too many relationship books are prescriptive and one-dimensional; The Relationship Status is not. Written with courage and humility, McCutcheon reframes our approach to singleness and relationships, calling us to something more true and beautiful than simply being in love with the idea of being in love.

Adriel Booker
*Author of Grace Like Scarlett
and (forthcoming) Tethered to Hope*

"The Relationship Status" is a must-read.
I couldn't put it down. Sarah's courageous vulnerability from her own story is refreshing and hits the nail on the head when it comes to creating clarity and purpose in the murky waters of relationships these days. There is nothing more valuable in life than understanding who God is and how He's created us to relate with Him and each other to be a part of His narrative. The way this book unpacks these realities, delivering constant truth bombs, leaves readers with a sense of dignity and empowerment to walk securely in their God-given identity.

Josh Cole
YWAM Leader, Tauranga NZ

Far from writing from the lofty heights of pretend perfection, Sarah opens her heart and shares her journey, one that I believe many people from different generations will identify with. Mixing her stories with deeply funded Biblical reflections and relevant cultural insights, she invites us to (re)consider relationships from the most important of all relationships, our relationship with God, to every other aspect in our relationship with ourselves, our romantic connections, our friendships, and our relationship with the world around us. I recommend this book to Pastors (and not just Youth Pastors!), to leaders, to parents and to young people facing the challenges of relationships in our time. I can't wait to read with my teenage daughter soon, and one day with my boy. Read it, share it, promote it, this is a treasure in your hands.

Rev Pablo Nunez
Minister of the Word at Ballina Uniting Church

To all my friends xo

An invitation to live the gospel.

CONTENTS

We are ALL called to love.

HELLO.

Everyone desires to love and be loved. We humans were made for relationships. So why do we limit our lives to just one type of relationship – the romantic kind?

For centuries there has been tremendous societal pressure within families, churches, and communities to be married. While marriage is a good thing, we have too often conveyed a feeling that a person is somehow incomplete or unfulfilled without a spouse. This is not a book about being single – or about getting married. It's about the value of relationships and living with conviction in your identity and calling.

I was never going to write a book like this. Then one day, I realised I had been writing this book my entire life. What began in conversations with friends (and sometimes random strangers) continued to stir my spirit until it poured across the pages of several journals.

This book could be called a journey or even a testimony, but it's not a formula or a doctrine concerning romantic relationships. I don't pretend to have all the answers and I don't have my own life entirely figured out. I am certain the answers we all need can be found by following Jesus and allowing His ways to become our ways.

What you will read on these pages is honest, real, and tested through my own life experiences. It is by far the most vulnerable thing I have ever done. I would prefer to have kept the relationship choices I have made private. I don't expect other people to understand all my decisions. Many are faith-based and have cost me dearly, but thankfully, they are decisions I don't regret as God has led me down paths beyond my own understanding.

While I hope you will benefit from what I have learned and experienced, I know each life is unique and every journey different. At the time of writing this book, a few well-known authors and songwriters who influenced my generation have publicly changed their beliefs. Some are now opposing the very ideas they once wrote about with such conviction. It's not surprising. Life has a way of confronting absolutes, and you must continually pursue truth so it remains relational and not religious. My story will be different from yours, but together we can share a singular and consistent truth – that we are all called to give and receive love.

Embracing this truth requires us to value others as ourselves and always points us back to the character of God. As you read this book, I hope it will lift your eyes to discover a good Father who desires to expand your heart beyond its current horizons.

From beginning to end, God's eternal dream for humankind has involved relationship. One day He will gather people of every tribe, language, culture, and personality to worship together before his throne (Rev. 7:9) in perfect relationship. Thankfully, we don't need to wait till the end of time to form loving, eternal relationships. If we love and worship God now, it leads to a love for others and a life filled with relationships that will impact eternity.

The church has much to do to reach her potential in modelling healthy relationships that go beyond romance alone. Too often, it has conveyed a narrative disconnected from God's dream for humanity. Instead of creating a community that embraces the individual, it has caused individuals to feel shame about not being married. Each of us (married or unmarried) has an honoured place within the Kingdom community. We are called as sons and daughters into relationship with a loving Father who commissions us to develop loving relationships across the globe.

I wish I had this book in my twenties when I was grasping for truth and trying to make sense of difficult situations. I was often given relationship advice that troubled me because it did not align with God's character and nature. That confusing time moved me to dive deeper into the Word of God. Over the last 20 years, I've devoted myself to discovering His view of relationships. Those discoveries form much of the content you will read in this book. I have learned that I am loved –in a way that I can know, feel, and experience. I have found that my life purpose is true partnership with God. This friendship with my eternal Father has proved more satisfying and valuable than any other lifetime achievement. It makes room for me to love others.

I invite you to use this book in your relationship journey with the Lord. Discuss it with friends and seek the Lord together. God has an abundance of love and relationships for you beyond what you could ever imagine. I dream of a day when churches everywhere build a Kingdom community that integrates social class, culture, age group, and any relationship status – providing a piece of heaven right here on earth. This will happen as we invite God to make His home in our hearts, as He empowers us to love as He loves.

After all, you were made for relationship.

PART ONE

THE REALITY

"Trust in the LORD with all your heart,
and do not lean on your own understanding."

Proverbs 3:5

CHAPTER 1

WHY AREN'T YOU MARRIED?

This blunt and unexpected question was thrown at me by a leadership conference speaker when I was 29 years old.

My friends and I were excited about this conference. Hundreds of young leaders from all over the country had registered to attend, and the list of guest speakers was impressive. The program was filled with worship, teaching, and workshops. Midway through the week, the event manager asked me to emcee one of the evening programs, interviewing a professor he described as an expert on Biblical Worldview.

I accepted the invitation and met the professor at the campus café. As we sat down with our coffees, our meeting began with the usual introductions and small talk. Everything was going well with our preparation until the professor interrupted with the 'dreaded' question. At first, I looked puzzled. His random change of subject derailed the entire agenda of our meeting. But that conversation became a tipping point in my identity and calling. It made me face all the secret fears I had about myself and the God I chose to follow with my whole heart.

Here's how it all began:

Me: "And then I will ask about your earlier experience on the mission field during...."

The professor: "Are you married?"

[Awkward pause]

"Um...No"

"Why not?"

My next awkward pause prompted the professor to suggest his own idea. "It's probably because you are intimidating. Have you considered that before?"

"Umm maybe." I tried to look casual but felt tears building behind my eyes.

"Well, have you approached any of the guys at this conference"?

"Umm...Does talking to your friends count?"

"Okay. Here's what you need to do. Walk up to a guy at the next coffee break and ask him about his view on worship. That's a good way to find a spouse."

Yes, this guy was serious. My mind was frozen, trying to understand why someone I had just met was trying to figure me out based solely on my relationship status. Within a few minutes, the professor had rendered me speechless. It also shocked me that this man would interrupt our meeting to suggest reasons 'why' I wasn't married. It was bizarre that he believed his advice would be helpful for me.

I began to wonder: Is not being married an urgent problem? To the professor, it was. He dismissed all my reasons for my current relationship status as invalid. During the conversation, I had flashed a desperate glance at the event director, who sat silent. A professional planning meeting had developed into an assault on my identity as an unmarried adult. Ironically, the evening presentation sought to inspire young people to say yes to following Jesus at personal cost. Now I was curious as to how the professor's question would reconcile with the evening's purpose.

Why was such a simple annoying question so difficult to answer? Was being unmarried in your late twenties so confusing to people that it needed to be confronted? Before that conversation, I had never thought that my relationship status had 'stood out' in this way. The thought that some people had this question in the back of their minds when they looked at me was deeply unsettling.

Why wasn't I married?

The mind can rummage through all your worst fears in a quick attempt to do such a critical life assessment.

Am I really not married because guys find women leaders like me intimidating?

Is my singleness a reflection of my character, my personality, and my calling?

Is my unreserved 'yes' to God disqualifying me from a romantic relationship?

This led to more questions about how people view me as an unmarried woman:

When I am talking to others in ministry, is that what they are thinking?

Are people going to listen to what I have to say if I am not married?

Does declining a recent invitation to a coffee date indicate I'm too fussy to get married?

The conversation stirred up insecurities I didn't know I had. It also opened my eyes to realise how obsessed with marriage we are in the Western Christian culture. Something switched on inside me that day, and it would not rest until I found the answer. But first I needed to confront all the lies I didn't know I had been believing. I needed to discover the truth about God's view of relationships. I would need to search, but the good news is that the truth wants to be found.

Leading up to that defining conversation with the professor, I had loved my life. It wasn't perfect, but I was living in the adventure of serving a big vision and enjoying great relationships with both friends and family. My life felt full. Although I still had desires in my heart, I had found contentment in the present and trusted God with the future. I did not feel alone, and until then, I had no reason to worry.

It shocked me that I could not articulate a reasonable response expressing why there was so much more to me than my relationship status. I left the professor interview feeling I had not been heard or understood. Why was my relationship status always so important to people? Is this my only place in the community, the only way I will belong as an adult? I had reasons for why I wasn't married and sadly, they were all perceived as negative. So one-by-one I explored questions I hadn't fully considered before.

"How does society view me as an unmarried person? How does my church view me? Is my identity somehow tied to their perception"?

"Does being unmarried determine my place in our community"?

"Have I missed out on something I was supposed to be paying attention to"?

And the most frightening question: "What if I never get married? Would my life have any less value? Would I be lonely"? Help me understand, Lord.

In my desire to love and be loved, there were times I had prayed for a husband and knew I was open. I considered myself available if God wanted me to marry and was mostly at peace with being unmarried until now. Another more serious question presented itself ...

Why do I want to get married?

CHAPTER 2

WHEN LIFE FEELS URGENT

Marriage was never intended to measure a person's value or their place in the community. People are unmarried for all kinds of reasons. Yet especially within the church, unmarried people feel a largely unspoken cultural pressure to wed by some point in life. Assumptions and expectations seem to rise the longer one is unmarried.

At first, I was unaware I had formulated an imaginary timeline of when I would get married. It was buried deep in my subconscious. When it did pop up in my head, I concluded marriage would happen by a certain age. But that age kept shifting. I first assumed I would get married at 24. Then I moved the timeline to 27, maybe 33, and then 38. Each deadline was always a few years ahead – just far enough so I didn't have to worry about it in the present. When those ages came and went, I gave up on the timeline and decided to live in the mystery. There are some things we cannot predict or control.

The life timeline does have some reality to it. Things such as education, mortgages, and contracts all have timelines. However, God's timing concerning relationships doesn't work like a transaction. We don't need to set a timeline in the relational process of trust. We just need to steward the present. God understands our desires, and He sees time differently than humans do.

I was in my early twenties when my mother was diagnosed with cancer. I remember sitting in that sterile medical office with Mum and Dad when the doctor spoke these life-shattering words. "The cancer is inoperable. At best, you have two years to live Mrs McCutcheon." Time seemed to stop as we each reacted to the news. My father broke down in tears. Mum, who was nearing age 50, started to sob too. Then she quickly turned to me and said, "You have two years to get married and have children."

I froze trying to process the fact that my mother would most likely not be there for the most important moments of my life. Moments that for me still felt far in the future. Moments that were not supposed to happen yet. I immediately felt the pressure of Mum's timeline. I began to think about my male friends, and if I would want to marry any of them. I thought of the times I had the opportunity for a serious relationship and had declined for reasons I now questioned. I thought about my sisters; none of us were married. What kind of future would any of us have if Mum wasn't in it? Dark and random thoughts surged through my head at lightning speed. The mind works fast when it is afraid. In seconds, the unexpected news about my mother had compressed my entire life into the length of two years.

Of course, I understood why Mum said what she did. Mothers and fathers have dreams and expectations. Important things. Things they are looking forward to. Mum's sudden outburst exposed a desire to see me married and having children. The irony of that moment in the doctor's office was that my parents had always encouraged me not to rush into marriage. I was 'not allowed' to date until I was sixteen. I think they were worried I would marry young. They believed marriage was for life and raised me to make a mature decision. I loved my parents, and their opinions mattered to me then. They still did. Mum's situation put everything in my life on fast forward, especially relationships. I suddenly felt jumbled and knew this crisis would test my values.

Hebrews 11:6 teaches us that God always rewards a true seeker. The text indicates there is something dynamic available for those who courageously go beyond the realm of general faith and into the vulnerability of personal faith. This faith holds the risk of an unknown outcome – a disappointment or perceived failure. It requires us to trust God in practice, not just in principle. For it's easy to have faith for things until your heart is involved.

I wanted to please my parents, but I wanted to please God more. Risk-taking faith often starts by asking for God's opinion on things that matter to you. It requires a willingness to yield control and trust in God's character. The Lord rewards those who stake their future on Him and pursue a journey of learning. A true seeker will risk being wrong in the pursuit of truth. A true seeker pleases God.

In Jeremiah 29:12-13, God invites us to call and search for Him. He wants to tell us things 'we do not know '(Jeremiah 33:3). To draw us close in relationship. The Lord does not fear our discontent or our questions. Through them, our soul is stirred into action. Our restless hearts search for truth, and this is exactly where God wants to meet us. It's the secret place.

God didn't initiate the sense of urgency I felt. It had come from my mother's heartfelt desire. Time is limited for us all, and Mum felt it more profoundly than most.

When things don't go according to our desires or plans, we so often ramp up the pressure on ourselves and others. In times like these, we must not allow questions about our relationship status to confront our value, our identity, and our belief in God's character. Worry and fear can unravel our self-worth like a ball of yarn.

We will be tossed around endlessly in an ocean of fear if we do not place an anchor in our soul. To find out if you are anchored, ask yourself:

Am I really 'alone'?

CHAPTER 3

UNDERSTANDING OUR CALLING

I grew up in an incredibly loving family living in an Australian country town where most girls married in their teens. Our town had many young families. I was the girl "most likely to be married by 17." It was just what everyone expected, and I would have agreed.

As a little girl, I was fascinated with brides, and my favourite toy was a glow-in-the-dark Barbie™ doll. To me, she was 'Bride Barbie'. Her fluorescent pink dress with giant puffed sleeves should have given me a clue that this Barbie was no bride. But it wasn't until years later I saw the exact doll on an Instagram account for '80s girls' that I realised my ideal 'bride' was just a sparkly 'prom queen' Barbie. The whole time she had been wearing a ball gown, not a wedding dress!

Bummer.

This newly discovered fact confirmed how obsessed with brides I was as a child. After my goodnight kiss from mum and dad, I would lay awake admiring 'Bride Barbie' as the doll's neon stars lit up her perfect blonde hair. She was beautiful, and I wanted to become a bride just like her one day.

In my childhood dreams, I wanted to marry a prince, or perhaps a warrior, or maybe even an action hero. My 'knight in shining armour' would change based on whoever was inspiring me at the time (Robin Hood and Batman need a special mention here). In my early teens, I settled on the idea of marrying an international leader. A man with a dynamic **'calling'** We would change the world together. Largely for that reason, I didn't date in high school. The guys at school couldn't compete with my dream guy. I was happy doing life with my friends and figured romantic stuff would happen once I was an adult.

What I didn't expect was that at age 17 I would discover a bigger dream for my life. I stepped straight out of high school into a missions training course that blew open my small world and exposed me to exciting new possibilities. It completely changed the way I related to God. During the course, I lived among and built friendships with students from several different countries and cultures. Together we learned about the nature and character of God and discovered He had vision for our lives beyond our relationship status. As my relationship with God grew, my desires began to change. The Lord was forming in me what I came to understand as my 'calling' – a deep sense of truth that would forever change my life. At the end of the training program, one of our directors presented a long-term vision strategy for our city. It was exciting, and I knew I wanted to be a part of it. That spark lit a fire within my heart.

I had once only ever dreamed about 'getting married'. Now I realised marriage was no longer the only way to live out my dreams. Opportunities came to start a romantic relationship, but I didn't want to go into one until I was ready to get serious. At the time, there was nobody I felt serious about. God has set a fire inside my heart. It consumed things I once considered so important and replaced them with what He considered important.

There is nothing wrong with wanting to marry, especially to marry someone who has a dream you want to partner with. The Bible says, 'He who finds a wife finds a good thing' (Proverbs 18:22), and we know God delights in and blesses a marriage. However, my story is about surrender. Marriage was no longer the main goal of my life. I wanted to give God my best years as a young person, so I happily surrendered my plans for the adventure of following Jesus wherever He wanted to lead me. The way God calls me to live is not a higher call than others, but it is my call and only I could respond to it.

Early in my life, I had assumed my calling looked a certain way and needed a certain person to make it happen. God was shifting my ideas, breaking my boxes, and growing my heart to see life from His perspective. Calling is fluid because it flows from relationship with the Father. It's about following Jesus. Being led where He wants me to go. It's easy to think that if we just ask God one big question we will get an immediate download of detailed directions for the rest of our lives. Honestly, if that happened, the immensity of it would blow our minds. We shouldn't expect a one-off instant revelation of our 'calling' or life direction. It's all about the process.

As I reflect on my life, I see a series of "saying-yes-to-Jesus" decisions that led me into many different roles, jobs, and titles. A true calling is not defined by a job, a platform, or a status. It has to do with developing your gifts and stewarding your life well. The call is listening to the voice of God and valuing His ways. I used to think that a calling was a career, but it is about relationship. I soon began to realise that God is way more concerned with who I am becoming (Christlike) than what I am doing. Consider the life of King David. He started his journey to adulthood as a shepherd, which was seen as a lonely, dead-end job. But while tending sheep, David learned to converse with God and create Psalms of worship. He also learned to be a warrior – striking down a lion, a bear, and then the Philistine Goliath. David continually developed his three giftings (shepherd, worshiper, warrior) and desired God to be the priority. By the time David unexpectedly faced his first giant when visiting his brothers, there was an immediate response that came from the overflow of a man who knew his God.

Through stewarding his daily life David became "a man after God's own heart" and eventually the King of Israel.

Psalm 119:105 teaches that God's Word is a "lamp unto our feet." Picture that image for a moment. You are walking with God step by step. As you take a step the next step lights up. This very image occurs as we walk with Him.

My calling has simply been the next 'yes' to Jesus.

This is often described in the church as a life of faith and obedience. The problem many have in understanding this concept is that obedience implies being forced to do something against your will. As children, we were taught to 'obey' or be punished. No wonder our hearts wrestle with that word. God's definition is different. He wants us to choose Him, to follow Him, and yes, to obey Him out of love. Jesus lived in willing obedience to the Father. Out of love for Him and for us, He gave His life to redeem us. When we are secure in His love, we too can willingly trust. He never forces us to obey. Forced obedience is not genuine love. Jesus desires so much more than obligatory tasks or good service. He wants our hearts. As I reflect on my life, I have had many roles and responsibilities. They are part of the call the Lord has given me. Each one has required ongoing responses of loving obedience. I don't obey God because I am following orders. I follow out of love and friendship because He has my heart.

The nature of Biblical obedience is relational.

CHAPTER 4

SO ARE WE REALLY 'SINGLE'?

It's a tag. A title. A social status.

The term "single" is often connected to the line 'ready to mingle.' It implies 'open game' or perhaps more negative connotations such as 'desperate' or 'lonely'. I have always been uncomfortable being identified as 'single' because I don't believe it represents my life as a disciple of Jesus.

Following the way of Jesus always leads to relationships. My story unfolded as I became who God created me to be, developing friendships and working in a dynamic team. That's why I never used the word 'single' to define who I am. The title simply didn't connect with my way of life or fit my social vocabulary.

There are countless books and social groups for unmarried people, but I was never drawn to them. They didn't seem important or relevant to my needs. It wasn't until my late twenties that I began to desire a romantic relationship. In my thirties, I was still content and confident as an unmarried woman, but I began feeling distressed after declining dating invitations – even though I did so for sound reasons relating to values, attraction, and calling. And though I had dozens of meaningful relationships, I suddenly felt incomplete because of the expectations of others.

When asked if I was dating anybody, a "no" answer unleashed a myriad of suggestions to assist my perceived lack in this area. These included "Oh, you just need to open up your heart more," or "Perhaps try to flirt a little so guys can see you're interested." Their suggestions were always more of this, less of that, and focused on helping me figure out what I was doing 'wrong'.

What is so 'wrong' with not being in a romantic relationship? Nothing so far as I could see. But obviously, it was a problem in the eyes of others. Sometimes I feared I would bend to the pressure and enter a romantic relationship to avoid having to deal with all these awkward and exhausting social conversations.

One day I decided I would no longer defend myself from these questions or unhelpful suggestions. Some questions don't need to be answered. A person's life should speak for itself. My answers weren't helping anyway. Once I stopped stressing about what others thought, I realised the only opinion I needed to be concerned about was God's.

But new questions flooded my mind: Could I trust God to guide me on this even when I didn't understand? Do I believe God will give me personal wisdom for taking steps towards a special relationship? Is it okay if I don't want to be in a romantic relationship right now? Does my trusting God need to make sense to everyone in my life? Are my choices honouring to God? As I pondered these and other questions, I slowly cycled back to truth that the title "single" is not a Kingdom concept. Think about the meaning of the word. The dictionary defines "single" as 'only one; not several'. Is there anything 'only one' or 'not several' about a life that is following Jesus?

Jesus modelled kingdom relationship by calling not one but twelve disciples. He called individuals onto a team and made them a part of something bigger than themselves. They spent time doing life and learning about the Kingdom of God together. When Jesus sent them out in ministry, He did it two by two – not alone. He commanded them to love one another, to love their neighbours, to love their enemies, to reach out in love to the nations.

Through relationship with Jesus, we are knit together in one family. "But to all who did receive him, who believed in his name he gave the right to become children of God who were born not of blood, nor of the will of the flesh nor of the will of man but of God." John 1:12-13

We are no longer alone. We are all God's children, formed into community not through marriage, but by relationship with God himself. Another metaphor God uses to describe his family is the human body. Within it are many parts, but all work together. Think about it. Some body parts function in pairs (two hands, two feet, two ears, two eyes), but other important ones are singular (one heart, one nose, one liver, one brain) And of course, huge numbers of nerves and blood vessels connect all these together. God created us for relationships, and a marriage is only one demonstration of how this can happen.

Marriage will never take the place of the community God calls us to do life with as the church. We need people and they need us. I love hanging out with my married friends, unmarried friends, older and younger friends. My friendships include a huge variety of ages, backgrounds, and personalities. There are 18-year-olds and 80-year-olds as each person is unique in their friendship towards me. This is the fullness of relationship we can experience in the church. I enjoy staying with young families on holidays and going out for coffee with unmarried friends who work in networks outside of my own.

The idolatry of marriage is revealed when people believe it is the ultimate model for mature Christians. Consider the lives of the three greatest apostles. Peter was married, but Paul was not. When Peter questioned Jesus about the assignment given to John, he replied, "…what is that to you? You must follow me" (John 21:22). He sets us on paths that will be different from those of others, even different from what we and everybody else imagined. But regardless of our marital status, He wants us to be connected to others.

A romantic relationship may be in God's plan for you, and if so, it's a beautiful gift. But a wedding is not when our life begins, and marriage should not be where we find our social or community status. Even if I get married one day, I will still need my friends, pastors, mentors, teams, and family in my life. That does not make me a 'social butterfly.' It makes me a well-connected, fruitful member of God's model of community – the church.

Living within this model is not easy. At times I have felt disconnected and lonely. I have been tempted to use others for romantic comfort as a filler for social gaps. But these moments pass when I redirect my heart to what really matters. I <u>choose</u> to follow through on the things God has spoken to me. I <u>choose</u> my values, and I <u>choose</u> my friendships.

After all, to love is itself a choice.

PART TWO

THREE STORIES - ONE TRUTH

"... and you will know the truth
and the truth will set you free."

John 8:32

CHAPTER 5

THE STORY OF JAMES.

Everything on my list.

I was at a birthday party with friends when we first met. We lived in different cities, and I was only visiting his. A year later we met again, and he asked me out for coffee. My friends encouraged me to get to know him. It surprised me how much fun it was to be with James. He wanted to stay in touch. I wasn't sure what that meant, but I nodded approval and decided to see what might happen. More than I expected! Over the next six months, he was relentless in the pursuit of a romantic relationship. I wanted to be friends but held back, frozen with anxiety and indecision. I couldn't figure out why. Was I was afraid of commitment or was there something else?

Deep down I wanted to be in a romantic relationship. I had never been pursued so clearly by someone with such great character qualities. He was everything on my list of what I desired in a husband. A strong Christian. A great guy. Similar interests. And he had an amazing family. It all made sense in my head, but I felt stuck in my heart. Why couldn't I just give this guy a chance?

As I would later learn, a hesitation to say 'yes' usually means a 'no'.

After months of long-distance friendship, I began to search for the courage to express the decision I had been trying to avoid.

Eventually, his invitation to start a romantic relationship came to me as an ultimatum. It was a clear "Choose my ministry or choose him." The "choose him" option included some wonderful things. Once married, we would live in a beautiful house. I would be provided for. We could start a family. I blinked back tears as he listed unspoken desires of my heart. I didn't doubt his sincerity or his capacity to fulfil such a promise. I just knew I couldn't do it on those conditions and pondered whether a ''no" to him would close the door to ever having those things in my life.

I wondered why I had to choose between marriage and the mission God had given me. That answer became clear through the stark contrast in the way the two options were presented. I knew what I had to do and that it was going to hurt. I was confident I was doing the right thing, but I hoped I wouldn't regret the decision later.

After making that phone call, I burst into tears. I felt like a terrible person even though I had tried to be honest throughout our entire friendship. The voice of fear told me I was throwing away a good opportunity for a ministry option I didn't really enjoy. The thought wasn't wrong, but it also wasn't the truth. The ministry I was leading was difficult then, and it wasn't something I planned on doing my entire life. But it was what I was called to do at that specific time.

More tears flowed as I thought of the hurt my answer could cause. His invitation was sincere and heartfelt. It had taken courage for him to be so vulnerable.

When I first met James, I was in a season when the Lord was reshaping my priorities. He was asking me to surrender the plan I had for my life and my ideas for how I thought it should unfold. The national leadership of the organisation I was working with asked me to lead a youth ministry I had helped to pioneer. It needed to be rebuilt, and I had prayerfully committed to do so. It was not easy. At times I wanted to run away. God was asking me to stand firm and be faithful.

The relationship offer was enticing because I wanted out of this role. I dreamed of another life. An easier life. A life where someone looked after me. Suddenly here was the opportunity. All I had to do was say yes. But God had clearly spoken about my calling for this season. I had been given a vision to pursue and already put my hand to the task. I had tried to figure out a way I could do both the calling and this relationship, but it wasn't going to happen with this person.

This was not a matter of choosing a career over relationships. There was something much deeper at work in my heart. A career would have been easy to leave. But a calling is not a career. Callings involve simple obedience and the way we live our life. In that painful season, I spent a lot of time meditating on John chapters 14 to17, in which Jesus instructs disciples before He goes to the cross. He struggled too with the mission his Father had given Him. He prayed, "Father, if you are willing, take this cup from me; yet not my will, but yours be done" (Luke 22:42). In some ways, I was learning to persevere as He did.

I don't think James intended to divert me from my calling, but it was the reality of the decision I would be making. It was more than choosing marriage or a ministry – it was about choosing God. It was about remaining faithful. Does God have my yes? Or are there certain conditions attached with my yes that can change depending on the circumstance?

This process may not make sense to some people. How can a girl who desires to be married pass on an opportunity to do so? Especially when the guy pursuing her is a solid Christian. Why not give it a chance? Because my highest goal in life is to do the will of God. I want to get married, but not at the cost of disobedience to God.

God gently showed me what a choice to disobey would cost. I knew if I moved to another city, no one was ready to take over the ministry. All the young people I had been discipling would need to go somewhere else. In time another leader could step into the role, but how much time would that take, and at what impact? The partnerships I had been creating in the city would be difficult to delegate. Worse yet, the young people I was reaching might never again engage in a Christian community. Some would walk away from God because the person showing them God's ways had bailed. Would

I be held accountable? The weight of responsibility was real.

One day I was thinking about these things and grabbed my Bible. As I flicked through the pages, hoping for some understanding or reassurance, I mumbled to the Lord "This is my life; what are you doing?" Immediately, my fingers opened to the book of Ecclesiastes. I stared as a line jumped off the page and straight into my heart. It said: Since a king's word is supreme who can say to him, "What are you doing?" (Ecclesiastes 8:4 NIV)

I had just asked the Lord those very words in my pain and frustration. I stared at the verse and read it again. Did God hear what I had just said under my breath? Was He really that present? It had felt more like a sigh rather than a prayer, but it was definitely a frustrated cry from deep within.

There are two primary Greek names for the "Word". They are the 'Logos' and the 'Rhema.' The logos refers to the God-breathed, written Word of God. It is the word for 'scripture.' Jesus is the Logos (John 1:1). One of my favourite verses illustrating the Logos word is Hebrews 4:12 where the Bible talks about the 'Logos' discerning the 'thoughts and attitude of the heart.' We can so often find ourselves unsure on a matter and the Word of God has power to cut through the confusion and bring truth. Every time we read the Bible the Logos becomes alive and active in our hearts and minds.

The Rhema word of God means "to give utterance." It is when the Holy Spirit speaks the living word directly into an area of your life. I had just asked the Lord what He was doing with my life. He listens. He understands and reminds us of what is important. So I began to read Ecclesiastes 8 again, this time from the beginning of the chapter. It says:

"Obey the king's command, I say, because you took an oath before God.

"Do not be in a hurry to leave the king's presence. Do not stand up for a bad cause, for he will do whatever he pleases. Since a king's word is supreme, who can say to him, 'What are you doing?'

"Whoever obeys his command will come to no harm, and the wise heart will know the proper time and procedure.
"For there is a proper time and procedure for every matter, though a person may be weighed down by misery." Ecclesiastes 8:2-6

Amidst my pain and confusion, I found great comfort in these verses. My heart felt both confronted and comforted. Truth has a way of doing that. The Lord in His lovingkindness was gently reminding me that He is the King of my life. Although He is my Father and friend, He is firstly my King. I had given Him that role at age 14 during a youth event. As a child, I had invited God into my life through salvation, but as a teen, I felt the Lord was asking me to fully give my life to Jesus. He wanted all my heart and that night He got it, especially when it came to starting romantic relationships.

God understood that my obedience relating to James felt like it was costing too much. Through the verses in Ecclesiastes, He was reassuring me that wisdom knows the right time and procedure. Wisdom has a lot to do with timing. There is a right time and procedure for everything, especially relationships. The timing with James never felt right. Though I enjoyed being with him, there was constant tension between a long-held desire of my heart and trust in God's plan for my life. It is so important to remember God's Word through those times of tension. The heart aches when we must let go of what seems like our last opportunity. In those times it can feel like there is nothing else to hold onto – except Jesus.

Ten years after the situation with James, I got a call from a young woman I had befriended back then. The conversation began with an update on her life. Then she reflected on her teenage years. She was part of the youth community I was leading during the time I decided to say no to James. As our phone conversation continued, she paused and said to me, "I don't know if you realise the huge impact you have made on my life." I felt tears in my eyes as she continued to thank me for 'just being there.' A lot of things in her life had been inconsistent but my presence had not.

As I listened to her heartfelt gratitude, I felt deeply honoured to receive such thanks. She was only 12 years old at the time of my dilemma with James. I wondered how her life would have turned out if I was not there for some of those critical moments. Then I thought of all the other young people who were involved in my life and had the opportunity to encounter God during those years. The Lord could have called someone else to walk with those young people during that time, but He summoned me.

Upon hanging up from that call I thought back over the major decisions I had made in directing my life –

especially in the last ten years. When God is looking for a someone to care about the people He cares about – I always want to be His girl.

This is what it feels like to be grateful.

I regret nothing.

CHAPTER 6

THE STORY OF BRAD.

Why not? He's awesome!

They told me romantic attraction wasn't that important. Feelings come and go so it's unwise to base a romantic relationship solely on sparks or attraction. But can we have a marriage-bound relationship without chemistry? I have learned this area is more important than we realise…

Chemistry involves way more than physical attraction. Chemistry is when you both just connect on a heart level. You 'get them' and they 'get you'. There's a natural flow when you're together. It makes you want to spend more time with them. What causes this connection is still a mystery to many social scientists, but it is real. If you have experienced it, you will know what I'm talking about.

I've seen good chemistry in leadership teams, work relationships, friendships, and marriages. I've also seen actors and musicians display a chemistry on stage that doesn't always translate to their personal relationships. Attraction is different from chemistry. Attraction sometimes leads us to get romantically involved with people we wish we weren't. Over the years, close friends have confided in their stories of pain and confusion, how they were attracted to people who weren't suitable partners for them. How they wish they were not attracted to those individuals and that they had allowed God instead of the attraction guide their decisions.

Chemistry can make a relationship feel right, but it shouldn't be the sole decision maker in starting a committed relationship. Not everyone we are romantically attracted to will be a good match for us. And the having or not having romantic feelings should never replace Holy Spirit's wisdom in relationship decisions.

I worked in ministry with a friend I highly respected. We were good mates and had been for many years. He knew my family. I knew his. He was loyal, kind, fun, and generous – a joy to be with. We both led youth ministry teams and had similar values. It was easy to trust him because he was a man who was always going to do the right thing. Everybody loved him. I did too, but I would soon realise it was not with a romantic love.

Friends thought we were a great match so I opened my heart to a deeper relationship based on their encouragement. I had no word from God and no romantic attraction. But I had hope that God would grow my heart if this relationship was His will for me. I began to feel a hesitation that wasn't based on fear, but due to a lack of romantic attraction and a sense that our callings were taking us in different directions. After a month of dating, I knew I needed to be honest and end things. I felt terrible. I wondered if I deserved anyone at all if I didn't want to date this amazing person.

God valued this man and had a plan for his life. Brad was not my 'gap filler,' but I realised that is what this friendship could become. My friend was worthy of being in a relationship with someone who adored him romantically and would partner with his vision for a country I knew I was not called to. This was not going to be possible if I was selfish. We broke things off, and I let go. Today he is married to the love of his life and has an incredible family. I am blessed to call both him and his wife my friends. I genuinely love seeing how committed they are to each other as they raise their beautiful children. Upon reflection, if I had not dealt with the reality of my heart and settled for a selfish form of comfort, I would have missed out on retaining a valuable friendship.

The breakup with Brad taught me a valuable lesson. It was the first time I understood why people try to play it safe in long-term dating relationships. It may sound selfish, but it is practical. He likes you, and you like him. Neither likes being alone. You each enjoy the attention of someone who cares about you. But without God's definition of love, you are just treading water spiritually. The Lord is calling us to a higher standard of integrity. If you're not sure about going deeper into a relationship, you need to ask God what to do. If fear is holding you back, He can remove that obstacle. But again, a continuing hesitation to say yes is usually a no. Love considers what is best for another.

It's wrong to lead someone on because you like the way a person treats you, rather than truly loving the person. Often people are so afraid of missing out on a marriage opportunity that they begin to make small compromises with big consequences. If your sense of security and identity comes from being in a relationship, you may never feel the peace you desire. You can be selfish in a relationship without even realising it. In hanging onto a relationship for your own comfort, you are hindering another person from pursuing the life God wants for them. Making the right decision is easier if you are secure in your identity, purpose, and values. It takes courage to choose the higher good by releasing that person to be loved by someone else in a way that you cannot.

Be careful not to rely too much on your heart in times of struggle. The heart can be deceptive and well-meaning friends can add to our confusion by saying what we want to hear. That's why we need God – who knows our heart. He wants to shine the light of His truth into our relational situations. His Word gives understanding and confronts selfish expectations.

I admired Brad. I wanted my brotherly affection for him to become romantic love. I didn't want to miss the chance to be with such an amazing person. But it never felt right. No matter how hard I tried, I couldn't make that kind of love happen. When our dating relationship ended, I was left wondering if I had unreasonable expectations or some deep character flaw. God comforted me through many months and many questions.

Understanding came as he showed me how He led Adam in relationship with Eve. In Genesis 2:19, God said, "It is not good for the man to be alone." Then he paraded every animal before Adam one by one. Imagine that scene for a moment. All those animals and yet Adam does not pick a suitable helper. Animals can be great companions, but they don't converse with us on a human level. The Father had the Trinity and the animals had each other, but Adam was the only created human being. He was still 'alone' in that there was no one else like him physically. After this lengthy animal presentation process, the Lord acknowledged the need to create a mate especially for him. A human being.

God was amazingly patient with Adam. His animal kingdom had supplied plenty of potential companions for Adam. This first human had met and named each animal, and he surely was in awe of God's creative power. But through the process, Adam realised that not one was the friend he desired. So God went back to work and formed one more creation. The moment Adam saw Eve, he knew she was his match and exclaimed, "This one is bone of my bones, and flesh from my flesh" (Genesis 2:23). Now I am not suggesting that God uses the dating process like Adam's parade of animals. My point is that God often takes us through a process so we can recognise His divine choice for us. He is a God who values process, and none is ever wasted with God.

Sometimes the relationship we desire will be years in the making. Some friends have told me they initially felt no romantic attraction to the person they later married. But as they came to know a person, to see their faith tested in crisis situations, and to observe their love and commitment, God birthed a deep love and affection. Respect along with love is a critical component in relationships. The romantic chemistry that often brings couples together may fade, but a commitment born of love and respect will grow deeper over time.

The way to navigate this kind of awkward process is with honesty and wisdom. I took a risk on a relationship that I thought had the potential to lead toward marriage, but it didn't take long to realise that he was more like my brother. I respected him deeply and knew he would be an amazing husband, but it was not going to happen between us.

Remember, having romantic feelings is good but also having the wisdom to choose the right life partner is better.

CHAPTER 7

THE STORY OF MARK.

When you take the risk and it doesn't work out.

Nobody told me you could love someone and not choose them. Nobody warned me that a romantic relationship like this could cost so much. Dating Mark would be the most painful experience of them all.

I was 31 when it started. I had been enjoying life in my late twenties. It had lots of friendships, and I loved my work building a missional youth community. My once-flaming desire for marriage had quietly dimmed.

Mark came into my life quite unexpectedly. After a year of working within the same organisation he approached me to start a deeper relationship. He was not my usual 'type' and came from a completely different life experience. Yet I was drawn to him. God had been challenging my romantic expectations, so my heart was positioned to be open.

Our lives were entwined through our work, so I thought I knew him. Even so, I took some time to seek the Lord. God gave me a vision of climbing a tall ladder leading to a diving board. In this picture, I was at the top trying to decide if I should jump in. It was a leap of faith out into the unknown. God reassured me He would catch me.

So I said yes and began what would be my first romantic relationship. It was at once both scary and exciting. There were times it felt like I was in free fall and didn't know where I would land. I was entering a process of trust and transparency I had never experienced before. I was getting to know and love someone, not knowing whether the relationship would lead to marriage or a breakup.

That is the risk.

The uncontrollable outcome.

The leap into the unknown.

I loved Mark. He was gentle, kind, fun, and talented. As we grew closer, everyone thought we would to get married. But after six months of dating, I quietly began to lose my peace. A deep conflict began stirring inside and made me want to hit the brakes. I wasn't sure if my concerns about Mark were valid or based on fear. The fear of the unknown. The fear of being hurt. The fear of taking the risk that love requires of us.

Several of our friends got engaged or married during the time Mark and I were dating. I wondered why we were not moving along at the same pace. A lot of my friends encouraged me to make a marriage commitment. Why was I slowing us down? There was a deep gnawing in my spirit that I could no longer ignore. Red flags were waving at me. I saw things in Mark's character that sparked hesitation. At first, I thought the things I noticed weren't that important. Nobody is perfect. We all have our issues.

You cannot know many things about who a person will become in ten, twenty, or thirty years. However, you can get a good gauge of what direction they are heading by observing how they choose to live their life today. It is important to observe the things that matter. What are their values? How do they relate to people? How do they handle difficult situations or conflict? What are they like under pressure? Pay attention to how he/she keeps their commitments or the way they treat their family. If concerns arise, ask questions. Sometimes the things you're concerned about are just simple misunderstandings. But don't avoid difficult conversations.

Pay attention to the red flags.

I'm not talking about little things that annoy you. We all have areas of our lives that Jesus is still working on. You're not looking for a flawless human because he/she does not exist.

A red flag is more about character and values. It can involve faith and your view on calling and relationships. Pay attention when they talk about marriage – especially their view of 'gender roles.' Listen, observe, and ask questions if something concerns you, but don't ignore it. That knot in your stomach that you hope will just go away urgently needs your attention.

Begin by identifying what you are concerned about and why it is important to you. Is it a real issue or just fear? Emotions are real but not always right. A red flag becomes a 'dealbreaker' when it identifies something you couldn't tolerate if it never were to change. Too many people enter a marriage expecting to change their spouse. That rarely happens because there is no grace for them to do so. A person's character springs from their own choices.

What a person believes has more to do with how they live their lives than what they tell you about their lives.

Observe whether your dating partner or fiancé lives up to the ideals they espouse and the promises they make. If not, you need to speak up. There is no peace in passivity. We cultivate trust by lovingly processing life's complex issues. And as you do, you not only get to know a person more intimately, you will also learn a lot about yourself. Work to address concerns early and always bring them before the Lord.

It's so easy to dismiss or ignore red flags when we don't identify them. Here are a few to consider:

What you see going on:

"He/she doesn't stick to their commitments or process with others who are affected by their decisions."

What you think is going on:

"He/she is not good at communication or may just be a 'free spirit'."

What is actually going on:

"We have different values and ideas about what is important in a relationship."

The one red flag I missed completely was how the relationship was affecting me as a person. As it progressed, I began to lose my voice. In past friendships, I always felt able to be myself. This relationship began turning me into someone I didn't recognise. My strengths and leadership giftings seemed like a threat to Mark. I found myself shrinking back, stifling my personality. When people asked for my opinion on matters, I toned it down. I became self-conscious of how my influence impacted the man I loved and his self-esteem. I would cringe if given compliments. I wanted to be in a ministry partnership, but I often found myself leading alone. As more leadership opportunities came, I backed down. I didn't want to create a shadow. I faded into the background, but the Lord would not let me stay there.

The anxiety I felt was not a fear of commitment. I learned long ago that commitment is the only way we grow. I would deliberately commit to plans, to decisions, and to important people in my life. Commitment was a 'muscle' I exercised regularly in my life. At that point, I had been with the same organisation working with the same team for fifteen years. So I decided to persevere even as things got difficult. I had used fierce determination to get through many challenges in life. Why not this? I wasn't going to quit on this relationship just because I had a few concerns. However, once again, the Lord was faithful to bring wisdom and clarity. God will always reward a heart that is genuinely seeking after Him.

One day my father came to visit. I had assumed he would be glad I was finally in a romantic relationship. My friends were expecting an engagement announcement soon. I suspected Dad had come to talk about that, but our conversation went down a different route. We grabbed a cuppa and sat outside to talk. Dad cut straight to the point.

"Sarah, the guy you're with is not good for you."

"What?" I was shocked. "Why?"

"He is not a good match for you."

I couldn't believe my ears. I thought he was joking and wanted to protest but the realisation that Dad had just driven hours to tell me this in person made the conversation feel much more serious. It had never occurred to me that my dad was concerned about the relationship. We had just spent Christmas together as a family, and I brought Mark for the weekend. I thought everything had gone well. Now I was scrambling for a clue as to why my dad sounded these alarm bells. He didn't criticise. He just kept saying, "You two are not a good match." My dad does not waste words. He encouraged me to consider the differences in our values. I said I would. That very day, I brought Dad's concerns before the Lord.

I soon realised (and admitted) that my boyfriend and I did not have the same ideas on what is important. The potential was there but unlikely to happen. It wasn't to do with our jobs or giftings, I just began to notice that things I thought were important were not important to him. Some things he wanted to do in life seemed pointless to me. I was carrying a high level of responsibility and he was still trying to decide on what to do with his life. We were at different life stages, and I had been waiting for things to get in sync. Wisdom began to whisper caution to me, but I didn't want to pay attention.

How important is this idea of calling? Maybe the marriage itself could be a 'calling'? I toyed with the idea that not caring about the same things in life was not essential if we truly loved each other. But that didn't make sense. I prayed God would change my dad's heart. I prayed that God would take away my concerns. I had grown to love and care about this man. I needed more time. I waited. But nothing changed.

It is a difficult, sticky place for the heart when you can't move forward, but you don't want to let go. One day I quietly prayed and laid down my concerns and expectations. I wanted to go "all in" and push my worries aside. I told myself we were in love and love never fails. I told God that if this relationship was not going in the direction He thought best, He would need to be the one to do something about it. I wasn't going to call things off.

Three days later, Mark broke up with me.

I should have seen it coming, but I didn't. It felt so sudden. Shocking. We didn't even have a breakup conversation. There was no process, no feedback, no answers. I felt a mixture of deep pain and silent relief. Although I knew it was right to end the relationship, I still cried for weeks and at random moments in the years to come. His hand was the first I had ever held. His shoulder the first I ever leaned on. He was the first person to change my relationship status.

God had allowed me to take the leap of faith into the relationship, but I forgot it was into the unknown. In the days after the breakup, I hoped it would be temporary. Immediately the Lord told me to 'let go.' I wanted to fix things, but God told me to 'be still.' I wept over those instructions, but the Lord held me steady. The words "let go" and "be still" came to my mind many times in the coming weeks as I allowed them to comfort my heart. I wanted to hear something else, but I knew I could trust the voice of the Good Shepherd. His leadership always restores the soul. So I let go and held onto Jesus. My peace gently returned but sadness remained present.

I have since learned that you can date potential; but you cannot marry it. You should marry someone for who they are, not what they could become. Because of free will, many people may never reach their potential; some never try. The vision you have for a relationship may never become more than a vision. I concluded that deep down I don't want to be tied to a person who is unwilling to grow. I want to become all that God has planned for me and steward this life on earth well.

Our relationship ended because the real issue was my boyfriend and I had different views on what is important.

And that is a big deal.

CHAPTER 8

DEALING WITH A BROKEN HEART

"The spirit lifted me up and took me away. I wept in bitterness and turmoil, but the Lord's hold on me was strong." Ezekiel 4:14

There are times in our lives when we can make the right decision but the ache in our hearts makes it feel wrong. This ache is because disappointment hurts. If we have entered a relationship with high hopes for the future, we grieve the lost potential of that relationship. Life was heading in a certain direction, and it suddenly derailed.

Falling is easy, climbing out is hard. Whilst I don't think I "fell" in love, love grew, and it was easy. Just like falling. You take the leap, and you don't know exactly what will happen. Going through a breakup can feel like climbing out of hole. You're shaken, unsure of how you got there, but sure you need to get out. God wants to pull you out of any situation you feel stuck in and set your feet upon firm ground.

In the end, I could see that it was right to end the relationship with Mark before it progressed any further. An engagement or a marriage would have created much more pain. Of course, it is tempting to hang on in a rocky dating relationship, hoping that patience and increased commitment will fix your problem. But if you are not in agreement about what is essential, it's already too big a problem.

From my experience, I can now understand why people did dumb things after breakups. There is a need to distract, to forget, to escape the pain. It was humbling to be so broken. You cannot push away the pain. A breakup is an end, a kind of death. Those who grieve sometimes fail to see a future beyond the relationship. But if your life is moving toward a higher purpose, there is grace for the pain. In John 16:20, Jesus speaks about "a grief that turns into joy." A pain that has purpose. A woman experiences labour pains, but when her baby is born, that pain turns to joy. Jesus endured the horrors of the cross because of the "joy that was set before him" (Hebrews 12:2).

The Bible also says the Lord is "close to the brokenhearted" (Psalm 34:18). One night I woke myself up crying out into the dark. As I sobbed into my pillow, I truly wondered if I would ever feel okay again. There wasn't anybody who could answer that question for me. During that dark night, I felt the Lord reach in and hold my heart. That image became a turning point in my sorrow and the only hope I found for that terrible season. Jesus is with me in the darkness. He understands my pain and can make all things new.

Be warned. Your heart may ache for longer than expected after a breakup. Mine did. But God is the heart healer. It took years for me to no longer wince when I heard my former boyfriend's name. Throughout this process, God reshaped my perspective and affirmed my identity. Jesus is my heart's true desire. Letting go of the relationship with Mark opened my life to new dimensions of Christ's love.

These three stories were powerful lessons about my identity and calling. Each was a unique experience. God's presence continually demonstrated His everlasting love and commitment to me. I am grateful for a God who, when trusted, can show me something better. God has thoughts that we are not thinking. I have learned that He is way more concerned with process than outcomes.

God does not play games with our heart, and He does not withhold good from those who do what is right. Sometimes, things in my life don't make sense, but I can always find the answers I need in the nature and character of God. He is a good God, and He always has the love we need.

Character, calling, and chemistry

These "Three C's" embody three critically important things God has taught me about relationships. I see the virtues of character, calling, and chemistry not as a religious formula, but as a standard for identifying what I would want in a marriage partnership. They are three things I am holding out for before making a covenant with someone.

I put character at the top of this list because we must never underestimate the value of character in forming a deeper relationship. Character eventually determines whether we will have low or high trust in that person. You are not born with great character. It is built over time through choices based on beliefs and values. If you are entering a covenant relationship with someone, you need to be confident in their character. It's not about finding someone perfect. It's about finding someone you can trust to do the right thing.

Obviously, calling is of great importance to me. I only want to be in partnership with someone who respects and supports my life calling. Likewise, I must be committed to respect and support theirs. There likely will be some differences in those callings, but there need to be significant areas of common values and passion.

Chemistry may seem like the most important of the three, but I see it as God's "glue" for connecting two people in emotional, physical, and spiritual ways they could never have imagined.

People often ask me to add another C for "commitment," but this goes without saying. It is often assumed that commitment is present in every marriage relationship. Sadly, it isn't. Commitment is a choice, a daily one.

PART THREE

THE CULTURAL NARRATIVE

"For I want you to understand what really matters..."

Philippians 1:10

CHAPTER 9

DEFINE 'NORMAL'

Whether we understand or agree with its standards, we all are part of a culture that shapes the way we relate to each other. The Oxford Dictionary defines culture as "the ideas, customs, and social behaviour of a particular people or society." I think a better definition is "whatever you define as your normal." Your culture (influenced by your nationality, gender, age, income, etc.) involves what is 'normal' for you, including many things of which you're not aware. Most of us cannot objectively see our culture until we step out of it and into another one that is 'different'.

You and I live every day in our own definition of normal. There may be a moment when we realise something is 'not normal' and we need to ask why. Usually, it's because our normal needs to align with God's way of looking at things – to adopt a Jesus-centred worldview.

This is a process. There are things that matter to God but are not yet important to us. When I began to make Jesus

Lord of my life, I noticed that my heart began to change. Things not on my radar before were suddenly of new interest to me, and they became important. When we allow His heart to come alive in us, the whole world becomes different.

Naturally, this relates to how we view marriage. The main goal of my life no longer is to get married – it is to do the will of God. If this involves marriage – great! But if not, also great! I have learned to trust God's ways even if I don't understand them. This attitude is not often seen as 'normal,' and I'm okay with that. There is a lot of freedom in recognising that sometimes your life choices won't make sense to others. There are no formulas – there is only relationship. There have been times I have wanted things that didn't happen, and I have not wanted things that did happen.

There are some 'normalities' in the church that we don't even realise are determining the way we view each other. Different wakes us up to see how our narrative is communicating what we value. Being unmarried is not a social condition that needs fixing.

Take for example the youth pastor on stage talking about his 'hot' wife. Perhaps the underlying motive is to demonstrate that God can be trusted to take looks and attraction into consideration when involving Him in the process of choosing a spouse. But there are other ways to give testimony to God's goodness without creating a culture that objectifies people and promotes romantic idealism. How we talk and tolerate what is celebrated in the church creates culture.

Once I was invited to speak at a church conference and sat in on the other guest speaker during his session. When this dynamic young pastor introduced his family with a photo on the giant screen, we saw a stunning wife with four beautiful children. Immediately I expected him to make a comment on his wife's appearance. Instead, he affirmed her speaking gift and other attributes. He said, "She is a better preacher than me." Then he shared about how they were both creating an incredible church community in an inner city. I was taken back at his comments. It took me a moment to realise his Godly approach was not what I had been expecting. I hadn't received his way of speaking about his wife as "normal," I am thankful we get to create 'normal'. The culture we are called to live is kingdom culture and this will involve change to begin valuing what God thinks is important.

We should be allowing God's truth to disciple us; not popular culture.

The dangers of comparison

We live in a culture of comparison. Even if we don't compare ourselves to others, it will be done for you. In my late teens, a friend and I started skateboarding. We got some beat-up old boards and began to skate around our neighbourhood. I loved it. Eventually we found the confidence to go to skateparks and use the ramps. I began to live and breathe skateboarding. After work, we would head straight to an abandoned carpark so we could skate for hours late in the evening.

One day I was learning to ride a half pipe when somebody publicly compared me to a more advanced skater. The comment suddenly made me self-conscious, which stole the joy of skateboarding for me. I wasn't trying to be the better than anyone else; I just wanted to have fun. I left the ramp and thought about quitting the sport altogether. Thankfully, I decided not to let the opinions of others spoil something I enjoyed. Others continued to make comparisons, but I just shrugged them off and continued skateboarding because I enjoyed it. I don't need to be the best.

Comparison is already deeply rooted in our culture. We compare cars, houses, universities, clothes, even churches. Some comparing is beneficial for judging how to get the best value on products we consume. But comparing people is <u>not</u> okay because we are each unique. This kind of comparison becomes a dangerous way of looking to others to find out if we are okay.

Here are some subtle – and not so subtle – ways we may compare ourselves to others:

- Bodies (She's so much slimmer than me.)

- Personalities (He makes friends so easily.)

- Talents (I wish I was that good at guitar.)

- Academics (Why do I have to study so hard? She excels at exams without trying.)

- Family (I wish my mum and dad were as nice as theirs.)

- Lifestyle (It would be so good to have that kind of money.)

We also compare things like social media followers, relationships, weddings, travel experiences, and the list goes on. It is easy to compare yourself to others, even if you don't do it consciously. Nothing good comes from comparison. It only leads towards two opinions, and both are negative:

1. I am better than that person.

2. That person is better than me.

These opinions are an attempt to measure worth and that is not okay. The worth of a person made in the image of God is a dangerous thing for us to judge. We have no grace to sit in judgment when it comes to a person's value. Humans have already proven that our definition on 'good' and 'valuable' is often framed within our own selfishness and this has lead to sin. We need to view comparison as a form of pride, and we need to be careful because pride comes before a fall.

Insecure people compare themselves to others because they do not know their own value. They don't understand how God feels about them. Even science recognises that every person on earth has fingerprints, eyes, and a voice so unique that they can be used to identify them. If God took such pains to create you in such a unique way, why would you compare yourself with another? You're not a clone. So don't fall into the trap of comparison. You will always lose.

Let the Lord tell you who you are and keep on listening.

CHAPTER 10

MARRIAGE AS AN IDOL

It's easy to wonder where you fit within the church community when it seems like everyone else is paired up. If we have a church culture that divides its community into "married" or "single" and suggests that singles need to get married, we are making marriage an idol. I know an idol is a strong word, but when something becomes so important that people will give up their identity and calling to obtain it, we have an idol.

In Western culture, we often dismiss the idea of idolatry because we don't bow to physical statues. That doesn't mean we have no idols. Idolatry can be a way of life, a value system, or an image we hold onto. It can be anything that takes the place of God, including out-of-order priorities. The desire for romantic love has become an idol for many. If you think this may be an issue for you, ask some tough questions. Are you willing to do anything to be loved? Have you given up aspects of your identity to date someone? Have you compromised your values or things God has directed you to do to adjust to their preferences? What dominates your thought life? Is your highest motive to please God or to please that person? Your answers will expose whether idolatry has crept in. If it has, repent, and ask God to resume His rightful place in your heart.

Sadly, love and romance are connected as the same in the minds of many. Even within the church, we have settled for a culture that exalts romance and marriage above other relationships. The social pressure of not being married, along with the feeling of not fitting in, has caused many a person to compromise on their values and callings to avoid being alone.

It is amazing what people will tolerate to avoid the fear of being alone. I know of people who have remained in destructive and abusive relationships out of fear of being alone.

We need to examine this emphasis in our culture seriously. Being "coupled" is not the only answer to the soul's need for love.

One Sunday morning I was invited to join a prayer team up front at a church. After the sermon, an older woman came forward for prayer, looking troubled. I had already met her and her husband at an event where I was speaking. I had found them both to be fun and dynamic. As we talked, she disclosed how unhappy she was in her marriage and said she had been struggling with these feelings for many years. My heart broke for her when she said, "I wish I had never married."

"Why do you say that? I don't know your husband well, but he seems to be a kind and godly man, and a good father."

"Yes, he is. But other than the children, we have little in common. I feel alone in our marriage."

"If you knew you had no common interests, why did you choose to marry him?"

"I was young, and I had this fear that I would never get married. He was the first person to ask me to marry so I said yes."

I tried not to look shocked about her explanation. I know so many young adults feel pressure like this. Their longing for relationship is great, and, if they believe it can only be met by getting married or living together, they will often compromise. I have seen people who were responsible for incredible ministries walk away from them to get married. It was not because their season of ministry was over but because something else took its place.

Another trap is to believe our calling will start once we are married. While Jesus encouraged teamwork (He sent out the disciples two by two), He never linked marriage to ministry. When we do, we may throw away the inheritance He has prepared for us. For marriage and ministry to work well, both husband and wife must have the same vision and values. As in other friendships, you retain unique aspects of your personality, interests, and giftings, but you have common ground on the things you both think are important.

How did we get here?

The church has rightly responded to the breakdown of society with the aim to strengthen and build better marriages, providing necessary teaching and dialogue on the value of marriage. However, the church has pushed this ideal toward idolatry. We need teaching and modelling on how to cultivate and value all relationships. Instead, we only get encouragement to get married and stay married. Not a bad topic, but marriage is only one aspect of the relationships we have been given to steward.

It is not wrong to desire to be married. Marriage as God intended is good. I love observing how it can develop character and create families. A marriage is intimate in ways a friendship cannot be. It is a covenant with accountability. I have seen many friends become 'better people' through a marriage.

I have also seen how the frills surrounding a wedding can distract a couple from the solemn commitment they are making. The engagement, the dress, the flowers, the wedding ceremony, the photoshoot, and the reception are all fun, but certainly not as important as the vows to love, honour, and serve. It seems to me that many young women today desire these experiences more than the relationship itself. The bride and groom are royalty for a day, surrounded by close friends and family, lavished with attention and gifts, and launched into a new life with a sexy vacation (AKA the honeymoon). But afterwards, they return to a new and somewhat ordinary domestic life that may seem like a letdown.

We need good marriages more than ever. I have a lot of married friends who share openly with me the highs and lows of married life. It seems to be one continual lesson on communication and vulnerability. It works best when it is fully submitted to God and anchored in the great common denominator of human relationships – friendship.

Getting proactive in friendship

I love my friendships, and I love to work with a team. I love hanging out with both married and unmarried friends. I am learning from the wisdom of both how to love God and love others more deeply. The term 'third wheel' is redundant when you have a couple who are both able to relate to you in friendship.

A good friendship requires vulnerability, generosity, kindness, and a genuine concern for others. Building rich relationships is a lifetime assignment from the Lord. Those who withdraw from other relationships to seek fulfilment in a romantic one will end up disappointed. They often bounce from relationship to relationship out of fear of being alone. Though they may love being in love, a romance will never fulfil our deepest need – a personal relationship with Jesus. He was a great role model for us in how to do relationships well. He loved and served and taught others with His whole heart.

Jesus was proactive in cultivating friendships and so should we. Don't wait until someone reaches out to invite you. Be courageous and invite others to gather for social activities. It doesn't matter if one person you invited can't come. Ask someone else. There will always be another person who is seeking friendship and your invitation may mean a lot. Don't just reach out to people who are like you. Get to know those who are unlike you. If you are young, seek out some older friends. If you are single, cultivate friendships with married people. Get to know people of different cultures and life experiences. Pay attention to details about their lives. Lean in to understand who they are and what is important to them. Giving your time to someone in need of friendship is one of life's most generous acts of kindness.

My greatest friendships did not come easy. They were forged through difficult times. Relationships need time to grow, and some of those times will be painful and inconvenient. But in such times, a genuine love for God will transfer into authentic love for others. Just look at how transformed Peter was after his conversation with Jesus about agape love in John 21:15. We see a different Peter in the book of Acts – a man who stepped forward to boldly face the same situation he ran away from in the gospels.

I once attended a women's event that organised the seating by tables. As it was about to begin, I noticed a woman from our church looking for a seat. I waved for to her to come over and join us. It was not a big deal for me to invite her to my table. But later that week she reached out to thank me. Her message reminded me how important something as simple as inviting a person to sit with you can be. When I extend everyday invitations to those around me, I believe I am helping fulfil God's dream for true relationship. Imagine a culture where we blend our status, class, and generations together to hang out. I think we would have something special that the world would want to join.

All the followers of Jesus have the potential to model heaven here on earth. We are all called to relationship as sons and daughters of God. In their book "Faith for Exiles" Mark Matlock and David Kinnaman observe that "the church can help fill a massive gap within our society...to be acknowledged for more than what we produce. To be known." (page 124) The authors research summarised that "Relationships are meaningful when we are devoted to fellow believers we want to be around and become".

The most holy and God-loving human to ever walk the earth did so with a tribe of close friendships. The life of Jesus was full of relationships in all their beauty, pain, and process. He ate with his friends, confronted his friends, and was abandoned by His friends and yet the same power that gave Jesus the ability to go after the one friend who had denied Him in His darkest hour lives within me. I can love like Jesus loves.

The church has the power to create a culture that builds friendships, engages true community, and inspires individuals to become more like Jesus.

We can do this!

CHAPTER 11

RELATIONSHIP FOR THE 'WRONG' MOTIVES

Working for two decades in youth ministry has made it clear that 'single" is not a desired title within the church. If we do not teach God's perspective on identity and relationships, we will continue building a church culture in which people will do anything to avoid being single.

Someone who feels confronted or shamed by questions about their relationship status can get trapped into unhealthy personal connections due to the cultural narrative. Consider the following quotes I've heard way too often:

"I'll just date this person so I am not alone…"

"I'll have a guy/girl friend that I treat as a boyfriend/ girlfriend until I find someone."

"This guy likes me and has heard from God about our relationship so I guess there must be something there."

"This guy has been pursuing me for a while. What if I don't get another opportunity to start a relationship in the future?"

"Well, my friends like him/her and everyone thinks we should be together...so why not just give it a go and see what happens?"

Any of these sound familiar?

In his book, The Marriage Builder, Dr. Larry Crabb challenges us to consider what we think we will accomplish from a marriage. The inner motive. The "why" we want to get married. The motive we don't think about but is there. Dr. Crabb suggests that everything we do in life has some sort of a goal and asks, "What is your goal when it comes to marriage?" This is a great – and often unspoken – question to consider when making a long-term commitment to someone. Marriage itself cannot be the goal.

Those who have made marriage a major life goal often feel a loss of purpose after attaining that goal. One way to build stronger marriages and to turn down the heat of cultural pressure to be married is to challenge young (and older) people about their expectations for marriage. Many think marriage is a way to meet their physical and emotional needs. We must remember that marital love as the Bible teaches it involves a lifetime of devotion and self-sacrifice.

In love with love

Sometimes we can just be in love with love and not a person. The songs, the chase, and the euphoria of attraction are all mixed in with the feeling of romance. A friend and I once spent a day walking around Paris. It is a city made famous by her poets, culinary appeal, and fashion designers. I love Paris, and I enjoy every visit to its avenues and tiny backstreets. Paris is known worldwide as the city of romance. Its commonplace to see proposals, weddings, lovers' picnics, hugs, kisses, and photoshoots. So many photoshoots! It is easy to bump into couples trying to perfect their selfie at the Eiffel tower or on many of the city's famous bridges.

Amidst all this activity, my friend and I observed a mix of ambitious emotional love and materialism. It was as if people were in love with love. Romance tinged with consumerism. We witnessed many couples splurging on fine food and wines, then going into expensive designer stores and coming out with loads of shopping bags. Often this was followed by a passionate public make out session almost as a 'thank you' to their partner.

The feeling of "falling in love" is an emotional rush. It's intoxicating, and as we all know, intoxicated people often make poor decisions. In that first giddy season, it's hard to discern between love or infatuation. Do we love the way that person makes us feel more than loving who they are as a person?

After a day of walking around in Paris, my friend and I sat down on the edge of The Seine. As we enjoyed a little picnic, we discussed the distinction between a love relationship and infatuation. In our experience, infatuation looks a lot like love, but its flame soon fizzles. It often starts with grand gestures that don't continue as the relationship deepens. Most romantic comedies are about attraction and the pursuit.

The reality of love in everyday life moments is probably not so funny or entertaining.

Behavioural Scientist (the study of how we make decisions) Logan Uri has observed how the unrealistic expectations many people have on relationships are a direct result of the way society has defined love through media. She says this has made 'romanticisers' of many of us. The romanticiser is 'in love with love' and believes that the hard work of love is in finding someone but overlooks the hard work that happens in maintaining a strong relationship. This adrenaline idea of love will not last. We are set up for failure.

This may not sound romantic but it would be helpful if individuals were taught character development and conflict resolution skills long before they were in a romantic relationship. The idea that we will develop great character skills on a wedding day is unrealistic. Just like learning a language, it takes time and effort to learn how to communicate well with others.

A great relationship depends on communication and learning how to lead our hearts well. Even if we have had poor role models in our parents, God can help us develop a new pattern of thinking concerning relationships. The message of Jesus is making us all lovers. That is the gospel.

An unspoken challenge

If a good friendship starts turning into a romance, the two friends will eventually need to decide together how they will define their relationship. There's no exact timeline for when to do this, but pay attention. Romantic feelings can develop with only one side knowing about it. If you sense this is happening, you need to talk about it before things get 'complicated'. When two friends have different ideas about what their relationship is, things can get complicated very fast. In the absence of honest dialogue, everything is left up to interpretation and personal expectations.

I have had a few important friendships that could have easily drifted into a one-sided romance if I became too casual about the time we spent together. If a relationship you're in begins to pick up speed, and that concerns you, the two of you will need to talk about it. It's better to either slow down or stop that momentum sooner than later. However, if this is the direction both of you want it to go, then relax and enjoy the process.

In my male friendships, I try to make sure my heart does not become so attached to a person that I would be heartbroken if he were to date someone else. That is honest friendship.

Anything else is probably not.

PART FOUR

A KINGDOM CONCEPT

"I pray for them all to be joined together
as one even as you and I, Father,
are joined together as one.
I pray for them to become one with us so
that the world will recognise that you sent me."

John 17:21

CHAPTER 12

A PLACE FOR EVERYONE

It was a beautiful summer evening, and I was seated at a table with a few friends from church. As we were enjoying a meal together, the host directed a loaded question at me. He asked, "Sarah, how do you feel about not being married when everyone else around you is?"

Suddenly all eyes were on me.

Awkward.

A close friend sprang to my defence. "Sarah has an amazing life. Her work touches so many lives. And she gets to travel often and do things that wouldn't be possible otherwise." I appreciated her sweet remarks and noted that otherwise meant "if I was married."

This question is a regular occurrence in my life, and I have learned to be ready to answer it at any moment. As the other guests shifted nervously, the asker of the question made it clear he still wanted to hear my reply.

"Thanks for putting me on the spot." I smiled. "I enjoy being together with married friends. But that's not really what you're asking, is it?"

Now it was the host who looked uncomfortable.

"Yes, I am open to being married, but it is not my main goal in life. Marriage is a beautiful thing to desire. I decided long ago, I was not putting my life on hold to make it happen or scrambling through options to force it to happen. I feel okay about not being married in my thirties because it does not define who I am or my social status. Marriage is not the only way to live a life."

I spoke with confidence because I know that is true. I can make the most out of my life in the kingdom of God married or unmarried. I can love at all times married or unmarried. If I were to marry, I would want it to be a partnership and be married for the right reasons – not because I was afraid of being alone or answering awkward questions on social occasions.

The person who first asked the question listened attentively to my answer. Other people began to dialogue on the topic and, as the conversation ended, the host challenged the very question he had asked and made a profound statement. He said, "If the church really is the family of God, then in God's family we all belong to each other as brothers and sisters." No one is left out. No one is alone.

I wholeheartedly agreed.

Marriage is not the passageway to find your place in the family of God nor is it the only way to build the church. Life together as followers of Jesus can look like family and is not dependent on any relationship status. At the beginning of that evening it hadn't occurred to me that I was the only unmarried person at the table. Afterward, I pondered on what it would take for the church to create a culture of relationships that brings people together instead of organising them apart.

In God's family there is a seat for everyone around the table and nobody is the odd one out.

In Genesis 2:18 God said, "It is not good for man to be alone." It is easy to assume that the opposite of "alone" is "married." Therefore, many arrive at the conclusion that "it is not good for man to be unmarried." But is that what God meant? In the beginning, Adam was literally alone as the *only* human on earth. So God created Eve and gave this new couple a mandate to multiply. In the life of Jesus (the new Adam) we see him born into a family, then bringing together a new family of disciples. These twelve (and later eleven), were transformed by Jesus, then multiplied into a much broader family of relationships called the Church. Though marriage is good, the Church does not depend on marriage as its primary way of growth.

Yes, it is not good to be alone. This doesn't mean you need to be married or to have someone next to you at all times. We should not be 'alone' in the sense of having no relationships. God's dream for you is a community of relationships.

A friend once sent me a blog of an Australian woman Rev Danielle Triweek, who did a thesis called 'The End of Singleness? Towards a Theological Retrieval of Singleness for the Contemporary Church.'

What a title!

She teaches that the unmarried single life although distinct from marriage, is uniquely meaningful and significant within the framework of eternal kingdom living.

What I like most about Dani's research is that she acknowledges the role of human marriage according to the Bible as an 'earthly reality that points us towards one aspect of the heavenly reality that awaits us'. Together we will be one bride married to Jesus.

However she also identifies how the value of human singleness (and celibacy) is an earthly reality that also points us towards a heavenly reality that awaits us (see Matthew 22:23-33).

Dani summarises this truth even more clearly in the context of the new creation by recognising that although marriage "points us towards the type of relationship we as the collective Church will have with our saviour", it is the unmarried life that uniquely "points us towards the type of relationships that we will have with one another."

Both are important and hold their own significance. Together they lead towards the fulfilment of the greatest commandment - loving God and loving others!

Wow.

When we focus on marriage as the only demonstration of Christian relationship, we devalue the unmarried life as a powerful demonstration of an age to come! It's time to change the popular cultural narrative of relationships to a kingdom culture.

CHAPTER 13

A CARING GOD, A CARING COMMUNITY

The first recorded miracle of Jesus (John 2:1-11) offers some amazing insight into how much He cares about us, even to the smallest detail. In the story, Jesus and his disciples are attending a wedding. His mother Mary is also there. Jewish wedding celebrations often went on for days, and it was the duty of the bridegroom's family to provide food and wine for the event. At this wedding feast, the family was about to face public disgrace because they had run out of wine.

When Mary learns about this, she quickly brings the problem to Jesus. He clearly doesn't want to get involved. He says, "Dear woman, that's not our problem. My time has not yet come" (Vs. 4 NLT). But He moves on behalf of the newlyweds anyway. Jesus takes water from their household jars (used for washing the hands and feet of guests) and turns it into wine – and not just average wine. The wine Jesus created from that dirty water was so good that the Master of Feast couldn't believe they had saved it to the end.

In Western weddings today we carefully manage our guest list and order preset amounts of food and drinks. There is an event planner, and if the wedding fails to meet your expectations it not necessarily a reflection on the character of the host. But in Jewish culture, failure to provide enough food and drink would shame an entire household and leave a negative mark against the newlywed couple for a long time.

I find it so remarkable that Jesus' first miracle was not the healing of a body or a supernatural appearance to His disciples to prove His divinity. It was an act of kindness to cover a couple's dignity. Even though it was not His time to do signs and wonders, Jesus decided it was important enough for Him to move on this family's behalf. Jesus gave instructions, and the servants and disciples witnessed a miracle. John 2:11 says this was the first time Jesus revealed His glory – and His disciples "believed in Him."

Jesus came to show us what God is like. This wedding story teaches us that God cares about our dignity. He understands social status. Jesus sees a need and meets it. It may be a need that seems trivial, one that could have been avoided with better event planning. But for whatever reason, Jesus cares. Even about the smallest things.

Jesus used so many small things and ordinary circumstances in life to teach Kingdom principles. He met needs large and small with equal compassion. There likely are things in all our lives that we don't take to God because they seem unworthy of His attention. He cares about small individual needs just as he does large community needs. What if instead of keeping these cares from God, we brought them before Him? I think it would give us the opportunity to witness the Kingdom in new ways and to learn what He sees as important.

You will see Jesus at work in your relationships. And hopefully, you will believe in Him.

A life centred in community

Jesus began his life on earth in a family. This was not the only way Jesus could have come to the world, but it was the way God designed, foretold, and fulfilled. When Jesus grew up and moved into ministry, he made a point to gather disciples by name and call them his friends. Jesus constantly did life with others in everyday ways. He ate, slept, talked, walked, laughed, and cried. Jesus was not married but attended a wedding. He may have had a desire for marriage at some point, but His greatest desire was to do the will of God. Jesus's life certainly did not lack relationship. People were drawn to Him. Crowds followed Him. People left their jobs and way of life to be with Him.

Our faith is one of community. A community that gathers, grows, and multiplies. A follower of Jesus will have a life filled with relationship. The fruits of the spirit include 'love, joy peace, patience, kindness, goodness, faithfulness gentleness, and self-control" (Galatians 5:23). These empower us to develop great relationship skills. The spirit of God works within me so I can learn to love others. This makes me excited to know God and make Him known. The great I AM created humankind and gave us a mandate – to fill the earth. A new way of living. A new system of values born from a relationship with the Father.

Jesus said the world will know we are His disciples not by miracles, good deeds, or achievements – but by our 'love for one another' (John 13:35). He prayed for us to understand how valuable this is and how much it pleases the Father. The condition of my heart towards another person matters because God is changing the world one heart at a time. He also helps change our perspective on what we see as valuable.

Seeing with His eyes

I was driving back from the beach with a group of friends when I saw it. We had stopped at a traffic light when the straw bag with gold stitching grabbed my attention. It was displayed in a second-hand boutique window with a small sign stating its price at $10. I didn't have my purse with me so I rushed home to get it. I drove straight back to buy this vintage prize. Sadly, the store had closed when I returned. I stood outside, admiring the bag through the shop window. I decided right then I wanted it.

The next day I drove back only to discover the shop was closed again – this time for the entire day. Once more I stood on the street and stared through the glass at this beautiful bag. It looked perfect. I imagined how it would appear with my different outfits. I had been looking for a bag like this for a long time. Suddenly I felt nervous. What if it sold before I could get back there again? The next day I phoned the minute the store opened. The shop keeper said she would put it aside for me, and I raced over during my lunch break to buy it.

When I picked it up, I realised why the bag had not yet been sold. The back side of it had gaping holes where the straw was broken. It would take a lot to fix it, and I didn't know if I had the skills to repair it. I had a decision to make. I held up the bag. One side looked perfect, but the other side was a mess. At that point, I texted a few photos to a friend who is a professional seamstress. She said it would be worth a try. I purchased the bag realising it would need work. I took it home and hung it on my wardrobe. It's still hanging there unfinished.

During this process I heard the Lord whisper an important lesson into my spirit. Sometimes we want something so bad we neglect to obtain His perspective about it. We convince ourselves we need it and make huge efforts to get what we want. Sometimes that happens with relationships. A man or woman will see someone who seems perfect for them. But they don't yet see what God sees. Huge hidden character flaws may be hidden behind a friendly, beautiful face. If we push for what we want, we likely will get it. But in the end, we may find we are not ready to have what we so desperately want.

The Bible says, "Man looks at outward appearance, but God looks at the heart" (1 Samuel 16:7). It is a gentle reminder that God sees the other side of something we want, and He knows what is best for us.

A mature Christian will face plenty of decisions in life, and those decisions should be based on what we believe and value. God has given us the power of choice, and our decisions demonstrate our devotion to Christ. He want to be involved in your stewarding of daily opportunities and all your significant relationships.

Take a moment...

Q. What does God think about my current social situation?

Q. What does it look like to trust God in my close relationships?

Q. How am I cultivating relationships in my life right now?

CHAPTER 14

MISSIONAL LOVING RELATIONSHIPS

God's command to love one another is fully inclusive. He loves regardless of relationship status, age, education, income, nationality, or other ways we humans define ourselves. We are called to do the same. Our love and unity must be modelled after His sacrificial love for us. No matter what our differences, His love knits us together as one family. And to use another metaphor, that love grafts us into Him, the True Vine. The source of life and fruitfulness.

Sadly, the relationship titles we commonly use have created some of the sharpest dividing lines within the church. The two main relationship titles are "married" and "single". Although some describe their status as "divorced" or "widowed" or "it's complicated," they can still fit within those two main titles.

Like most titles or roles, the word "single" generates unspoken assumptions. Many assume that everyone who is single wants to get married and everyone who is married has moved forward in their life, leaving their "single ways" and single friends behind. This 'great divide' (as I like to refer to it) also categorises people as "taken" or "available." This is not a godly perspective of relationships.

As Christians we are called to renew our mind, to leave behind the world's value system and to embrace God's value system. To put it simply, we change our old way of life for a new normal. This process begins when we repent of our sins and receive Jesus. This change of heart enables us to know God and understand His ways. Relationship with God is literally transformational.

I love how Jesus related to people of all kinds. He sat talking with a Gentile woman at the well. He was not threatened by her disreputable social status or shamed when his friends saw them talking. Jesus was friends with Mary and Martha not just their brother Lazarus. He showed kindness to orphans and outcasts and people in bondage to sin. He called individuals by name and made them feel valued. He still calls people by name today and welcomes them into His faith community. We need community because it gives our faith integrity. I can say I love others but, until I am living and working with others, my actions don't get challenged to match my words. I can only say I love when I am given the opportunity not to love.

The love God described in 1 John goes beyond affection and into self-sacrifice. It is a love I choose. A love that is given at personal cost and in many ways unfair. I cannot do love like this without the Lord's help. It is a love developed and tested through community. Whether married or unmarried we are called to do life together. We need the inconvenience of others in our lives because we grow in maturity and character from being in these relationships.

When God created Adam, he said, "It is not good for the man to be alone." We sometimes assume that "alone" meant "unmarried" because God created a spouse for him. However, in biblical context, God said it was not good for Adam to be alone because Adam was literally the only human being on earth. God's new creations of man and woman were given a mandate to "fill the earth."

In the New Testament we don't see Jesus making a mandate to find wives for all the disciples. Jesus becomes the new 'Adam' and demonstrates God's dream for humanity by gathering community for a purpose – bringing the whole earth back into relationship with God. In perhaps the most dynamic time in Christian history, the community of believers in Acts shared everything they had and did life together. So how is it that today we have divided the Christian community into two categories – married or single?

There is a whole realm of friendship we undervalue and forget to develop because we only think in pairs and are not yet community minded. If we think "being loved" is connected to "being married," we are missing God's heart for Christian community.

I have never described myself as 'single,' and it was never the way I saw myself. The word just never felt right with the way I live my life. Single is not descriptive of my calling, and it is certainly not how I feel. My life is not alone or isolated. I am an individual, but so is a married person. I am accountable. I work in a team and live with housemates. I seek the counsel of others in my decision-making process.

I find it interesting that marriage wasn't introduced until Adam needed "a helpmate" to complete his vocation of stewardship. They were joined together for a purpose. To fill the earth. To create more relationships. The sad turn of events in Genesis 2 with Adam and Eve's disobedience did not change who God is. God created mankind for a purpose. It's a big-picture, relationship-based purpose that remains to this day.

In God's kingdom nobody should be alone.

Affirmation and inspiration

God has a unique role for you in His Kingdom. As the Apostle Paul stated, "Only let each person lead the life that the Lord has assigned to him, and to which God has called him" (1 Corinthians 7:17). We are given roles and responsibilities connected to our giftings, our callings, and our level of faith.

While we are to avoid comparisons, we do need to notice and affirm the character we see in those around us. Why? Because Jesus did. Youth With A Mission pioneer Joy Dawson once described Jesus as "the most radical affirmer of all time." Think about the people he affirmed – a Roman Centurion, a tax collector named Zaccheus, the prophet John the Baptist, a woman who anointed his feet, and his perceptive friend Peter. We all need affirmation in our life, and we need to follow the model of Jesus in the way we give it.

I have made a point to be generous in affirming the strengths I see in others. This value doesn't threaten my own measure of worth. We do no favours to anyone if we are jealous, shy, or insecure in relationship to others. This small thinking hinders our ability to fully become ourselves and robs us of the influence we could have with others. Affirmation imparts blessing and courage. It empowers others to do the same.

I love to celebrate people. I love to call out the good I see in them because sometimes they cannot see it for themselves. I am grateful for those who have done this for me, and I understand its power.

Inspiration is another thing we all need. How do I know? Because the Bible encourages us to model our lives after great men and women of faith. Hebrews 11 is a great summary of these heroes. There are countless others in Christian history. Be looking for others in your own circles of relationship.

When I meet men or women living fully in their identity and calling, their faith and passion challenge me to greater levels in my own life. I do not compare my life to theirs or compete with them. But I admire the way they are pursuing their call. Such men and women stir me forward.

So instead of walking in comparison, acknowledge the good you see in others and allow that to inspire you to become all God has made you to be.

Take a moment...

Q. How has comparison occurred in your life?

Q. Why are missional loving relationships important?

Q. What are some ways you can affirm others?

CHAPTER 15

BUSTING SOME MYTHS ABOUT 'SINGLENESS'

MYTH #1: IF YOU ARE NOT IN A ROMANTIC RELATIONSHIP, YOU ARE ALONE. UNLOVED. NOT CHOSEN.

If you believe that the opposite of being married is being alone, then you probably assume that if you are "single" you are destined to be alone or at worst unloved. That is not God's view of our identity, and we must face the fear of being alone and deal with the lies behind that fear. Our value in God's eyes is never based on relationship status.

We were made in the image of God, and we were chosen before we did anything to deserve His love (1 Peter 2:9, Ephesians 1:4-5). God's greatest commandment challenges us to love others as He has loved us. He has chosen to be in relationship with you, and He will love you in just the way you need. His is the most important relationship of your life.

There are people in your life that God has already entrusted to you. They are your family, your friends, your workmates, your church, and your neighbours. Build those relationships and be faithful with the people God has placed in your life. It is not good for you to be alone, but that doesn't mean you should be engaging in a romantic relationship. Even when in a committed relationship you will still need friends, mentors, family, community, etc.

MYTH #2: IF YOU REALLY LET GO THEN "IT" WILL HAPPEN.

There is no magic formula with God. Just as each person is unique, so is their journey. There may be many times of "letting go" as you cultivate the discipline of surrendering your will to God. Letting go of hopes and expectations related to relationships is particularly hard. It can send us into an emotional free fall, cause us to compromise, or try to make deals with God. We must trust God in times like these. He knows your heart. He also knows timing. He may give instruction for you to position your heart or take action, but it will never involve striving or manipulation.

Things that are born of the flesh are sustained by the flesh but things that are born of the spirit are sustained by the spirit. We want to grasp for control, but relationships are not ours to control. You may need to let go several times – and to ask God what that looks like for you personally. We cannot manipulate God, and we shouldn't want to. A heart that knows God is good will anchor on this truth, even in distress. Sometimes the thing we think we want is not what we need at all. So letting go of a relationship is no guarantee that God will somehow restore it to us at another time. God likely is guiding you toward something better.

True surrender requires decisions to allow God to lead you into the unknown. Surrender requires the heart to yield. It is a position of being open handed. It is letting go. This may be seen as a position of loss but it is a position ready to receive. God wants to be the leader of our lives because His ways are wise and lead to abundant life. A friend once told me "Whatever we control we kill." It's a remarkable statement, and I think it shows the importance of living in an open-handed way. In a healthy relationship, you can't be in control, and that should never be the goal.

MYTH #3: ALL THE GOOD MEN/WOMEN ARE TAKEN.

This myth is based on observations made about people in healthy marriages. A mature married person is likely to reflect qualities we are looking for in a marriage partner. But consider this: That person didn't enter the marriage with all those good qualities. God used marriage to shape and refine their character. A godly marriage is good for individuals. It can make us better humans because making a lifetime commitment (involving vows and witnesses) challenges us to grow in new ways. Although we can mature within friendships, teams, and families, the covenant of marriage requires a whole new level of self-sacrificing. The deception within the "all the good ones are taken myth" is the idea that you should only marry a fully mature person. Look for a heart after God, maturity comes later.

The other problem with this myth is that it leads towards the fear of missing out. The Kingdom of God is not a Boxing Day sale (aka "after Christmas sale"). You don't need to push people aside so you don't miss out on a good spouse. Remember that Jesus performed his first miracle by providing the best wine for last. This miracle came from a God who was concerned for a newlywed's dignity at no benefit to His own. What does this tell you about God? Do you not think that He is also concerned for your dignity? Only God can save the best for last.

I do not why some people with a desire for marriage wait so long. But I do know that God is good and wise, and able to walk you through this. Having to wait longer than others is not a reflection of your value as a person. It says in Genesis 29:20 that Jacob worked seven years to marry Rachel "but they seemed like only a few days to him because of his love for her." Rachel was loved the most although she had to wait the longest.

MYTH #4 YOU SHOULD BE MARRIED BY NOW

We all come from different social norms. What is considered normal for your family, your church, and your culture can be different as time passes. I grew up in a country town where it was normal to get married before 18 years of age. I moved to a city where it was normal to get married in your 30s. There are all kinds of pressures, opinions, and realities on the topic of when you should "settle down." Within these is an inference that singleness is a waste of life. Again, that is not true. Don't yield to the pressure of someone else's marriage deadline.

Some of us may live an unmarried life, but it is not an alone kind of life. God knows our longings for love and connectedness. For women desiring a family, there is the additional pressure of the 'biological clock.' God is with us in all those times and honours those who allow Him to lead in the way He thinks is best.

A life led by the Lord may involve suffering and surrender, but there is an eternal story at play. God wants to reveal His heart to you for the bigger picture. I am always comforted by Psalm 27:13 which encourages us to see God's goodness in the land of the living.

Ask God to open your eyes to His goodness. It's there.

PART FIVE

LIVING FOR ETERNITY

"He has made everything beautiful in its time.
He has also set eternity in the human heart;
yet no one can fathom what God has done
from beginning to end."

Ecclesiastes 3:9

CHAPTER 16

A LITTLE PIECE OF HEAVEN

One balmy summer afternoon, I was delighted to be welcomed at a surprise dinner party. Our host planned every detail of this stunning feast. She seated us at a beautifully decorated table under a giant tree. The food was catered from the best cafe in town, and local musicians were hired to perform for our small party.

The picture-perfect event was a special thank you to those who had walked with my friend through a painful season. She arrived in Australia emotionally wounded after her long-term boyfriend broke off their relationship. We all stood with her, processing her pain through months of tears mixed with laughter. Beautiful friendships were forged through that fiery trial. My wounded friend felt loved and supported during that time and she was.

During that terrible time my friend met Jesus. I will never forget the incredible joy on her face when she told me she had embraced Him as her true friend and Saviour. Her eyes now glistened love instead of heartbreak. This is the way we were created to be.

You and I were made for a love that does not leave us. This dinner party demonstrated a powerful message about relationships that we rarely talk about. Love is more than romance. The true romance of the gospel is making us all lovers.

This story of my friend is one of my favourite memories because it was a little piece of heaven experienced here on earth. God has a beautiful way of working things out for our good. His redemptive plan has already put eternity in our hearts. The eternal gift of relationship with Him is a love that never fails. All of this is a gentle reminder that we are a part of something much bigger than our present.

The writer of Ecclesiastes reminds us in Chapter 3 that our times and seasons are set against the backdrop of eternity. Here on earth, some moments seem to take a long time and others speed by. It's hard for us to conceive of life that isn't marked by hours or days. But that's eternity.

Some of us freak at the idea of forever. The thought of doing something endlessly may sound exhausting. It did for me. However, I have learned that eternity is being fully present with God. He who describes himself as the 'GREAT I AM' The God of light and life and love.

For me the closest experiences I have had with heaven are when I have been seated around a table with people I love and who also love Jesus. In God's family, each person is connected by His Spirit. Through tears, laughter, sharing, prayer, and play we develop bonds even closer than our biological families.

One summer my friend and I went to the beach together and spent the entire afternoon talking and swimming until the sun went down. The sky turned pink, and the stars came out before we realised the time. The afternoon had turned into evening, but it didn't matter. We were enjoying life together and it seemed as though time stood still in each other's company.

On another occasion, I joined some friends in leading a prayer and worship event. You could feel the excitement in the air as the people gathered. The first song launched us into immediate gratitude and celebration. Praise and joy filled the room. Hours passed as we sang, danced, prayed and enjoyed worshipping a good God. If you had have told me beforehand that we would be on stage for five hours straight I would have felt tired just thinking about it. Yet when it happened, I had no sense of the time. When you are fully present with God and his people, everything else fades away.

I think moments like these are a glimpses of eternity. The dinner party, the beach hang, and worship afternoon are all moments when I lost track of time. Eternity is different from 'forever' because eternity won't feel like a long time. God is at work from beginning to end. He is personal and present working all things out in a beautiful way we don't yet fully understand.

Ecclesiastes 3:11 says God has put eternity in the hearts of man but "nobody can fathom what He is doing from beginning to end." This is such an interesting concept. We are set in a world we will never fully understand. But through its many different seasons, God is always with us. He is at work. He is present. He has a right time for everything. There is beauty in trusting God to work all things together for good with any situation (even when it makes no sense in my head).

I see eternity in people's hearts at funerals. I also see eternity at birthdays, weddings, graduations, and family reunions. These bring together family and friends from different ages and backgrounds. We may be laughing, crying, or sharing our hearts but we are together. That is what makes the moment beautiful. As an introvert, it may surprise people that I enjoy spending time with so many others, but this is the stuff of life. We were made to relate and not just with those who are like us.

My friend's relationship pain illustrates how we gain perspective on our life through a crisis. A crisis can confront what we believe and cause us to cry out to God. I think these are make it or break it moments. Will we pull back away from a God we don't understand or will we push into a search for truth? God is especially present with us in these moments.

One of my favourite stories in the Bible is a conversation between God and the prophet Elijah. You can find the story in 1 Kings 19:13-14. Elijah just experienced an incredible victory in a spiritual battle with 400 priests of Baal. Elijah demonstrated the power of God in a way that proved His God was the true God. However, despite this victory, Elijah flees in fear at the death threats of the evil Queen Jezebel. God finds Elijah hiding in a cave, fatigued and depressed.

The first thing God does is ask Elijah what he is doing. The Lord knew very well what Elijah was doing. God asks us questions not for information, but to connect relationally. He wants to approach our heart. God listens as Elijah complains that he is "the only one left" in Israel who is still following God. Then God casually mentions that there are 7,000 others in Israel who have never bowed to Baal.

God's perspective can be 7,000 times better than ours when facing our darkest day. We so desperately need His perspective on our reality. God is calling us to be part of a story that is far bigger than we could imagine.

One day we will stand before God and give an account to our lives. (2 Corinthians 5:9-10) I certainly don't want to reach the end of my life before realising that my priorities were all mixed up and didn't matter anyway. Life is too valuable to allow the voice of fear to dictate the shape of my heart and the direction of my life. I may have a limited perspective here on earth, but I have been given the opportunity to gain God's long term point of view through my relationship with Jesus.

Jesus' human perspective on earth could have tempted him to settle for what Jewish society expected of him, for what his mother wanted from him, or what his own friends needed him to do. Satan was constantly testing him. The Bible says Jesus was 'tempted in every way, just as we are – yet he did not sin' (Hebrews 4:15). Jesus overcame through faith and trust in a God who was making all things new. This is why Jesus is able to empathise with our human condition.

Through Him, God has placed eternity within our hearts.

CHAPTER 17

DESIRE OR DESPERATION?

There is a home video of 8-year-old me calling out to my dad at a parade during a World Expo event. My father avoids turning the camera away from the performance as he captures musicians, people on stilts, and dozens of colourful performers passing by. In the background you can hear my tiny voice persisting, "Daddy, please film me with her." When he finally directs the camera my way, I'm standing beside a mannequin woman dressed in a sequinned wedding gown. I am not even facing the parade.

Excited that my dad is finally filming the most important thing at the Expo, I begin to explain how this dress is made, admiring its details. I get a few moments of screen time before Dad goes back to filming the parade. When our family watches this video together, we laugh at the contrast between my father and tiny me. That 1980s wedding dress has long since passed out of fashion. This video exposes a desire of my heart throughout my childhood. I loved brides, and I wanted to grow up and be one. To be a bride was to be beautiful. It was a sign you were loved.

Deeper than all other desires is the desire to be loved. Chosen. Celebrated. This is humankind. Bride or groom. Male or female. There are desires that live within our hearts, and they are demonstrated in the things that hold our attention. Humans have a genuine desire for loving relationship. It is not something we should hide away in shame or hope that one day we will 'get over.' It is a desire directly from the heart of God for us to be in relationship – firstly with Him and then with others.

Psalm 139 affirms that God already knows the deep desires of our hearts. He sees through all the masks we wear and the things we pretend not to care about. He already understands what drives our deepest sense of self. When Jesus taught the disciples to pray, He began by approaching God as a loving father. Unlike the dismissive responses we may get from our earthly fathers, God the Father always welcomes us. Even when our desires don't seem spiritual enough for His attention, God wants to talk to us about them.

In my late twenties, when a desire for marriage began to emerge, I pushed it away. For a long time, I wasn't honest with God about this desire. I didn't want to become 'desperate'. I had seen people become consumed with the need for marriage, and I found it unattractive. I didn't want to become someone who surveyed people as marriage options. I then discovered the difference between 'desire' and 'desperate'. One begins with honesty of the heart, and the other strives from a sense of lack. Desire is simply wanting something to happen. Desperate comes from the Latin word *desperatus* meaning 'deprived of hope'. I know which position I prefer.

I love the story of Hannah in the Bible (1 Samuel 1). She was the favoured wife of Elkanah. He loved Hannah, but she still had an unfulfilled longing for a child of her own. She went to the temple and poured out her heart to the Lord. Her soul groaned with longing, and God heard her. Others heard her too. The priest Eli falsely assumed she was drunk, but God knew the truth. He responded to her plea. She left the temple knowing God had answered her prayer for a son.

Hannah had vowed she would dedicate the child to the Lord. When her son Samuel was of age, she followed through on her commitment. It must have been difficult for Hannah to give away something she wanted so much. Her decision was rooted in her trust in God. I think the best part of her story is that she was not left empty in keeping her promise. God gave Hannah and Elkanah five more children. This is what God is like. He did not fulfil her desire only to take it away again. He had a bigger picture in mind. A leader for Israel. A boy that was an answer to a mother's desire for a son was also the answer to a nation's need for a leader. God is faithful. He is generous. He listens and cares. goes beyond our perspective because He is at work in ways we sometimes cannot comprehend.

God can be trusted with the desires of our hearts. He does not mock or misunderstand. It is when we get real and raw that God answers or reshapes our desires. Some of my desires have been met and some have dissolved. I am still talking to the Lord about others. This is relationship.

This desire for marriage hits me at times when I least expect it. Some thoughts I ponder, and others I dismiss. Some fade during the day, then wake me up in the night. It takes discipline to keep my heart open and not allow my thoughts to slip into worry about tomorrow. It is an effort to remind myself of what is important. When I pause and take an account of my life from a kingdom perspective, I always find gratitude. The Lord has filled my life with good things. I love all my relationships. I love my vocation, and I love growing into the person I am still becoming. I am still learning, and the older I get, the more I realise there is still so much to learn – and at times unlearn. I have developed a great love for young people, refugees, and children. This does not diminish my desires, but it does engage my heart and fill my life with good things.

Tell God how it feels

Getting real with God about an unfulfilled desire is so important. God is not afraid of our feelings, and He does not turn away. Honest conversations with God will build your faith. As an Australian, it is typical in our culture to hide our feelings, put on a brave face, and carry on. I once believed that mature Christians reach a point where they could live in a constant state of emotional neutrality. No sadness, no anger, or any negative emotion. The Lord corrected me on this view. He reminded me that I am made in His image – a God who has emotions. I have learned to pour my heart out to the Lord, and I have found His gaze comforting. Sometimes we hide how we feel about an issue until it seems tidy enough to talk about. We ache inside instead of being honest with God.

This is not faith. Godly faith does not deny reality or attempt to run away from it. It is not based on religious formulas or fatalistic prayers. Real faith is relational and goes after God's heart. It is stirred by a desire to know what He is like and reconcile our doubts with His truth. This kind of faith seeks God's opinion. It is vulnerable. It risks letting go to gain something better.

Maybe you've thought, I don't need to get real with God since He already knows what I am thinking. This idea of God can keep us silent. Whilst God does know all things, any good relationship involves communication. God speaks, listens, and asks questions. Throughout the Bible, God is seen constantly asking people questions, and not because He doesn't know the answers. He asks questions because He wants to connect with our hearts. This is a God we can be close to. A God we can trust. Through honest communication, we build intimacy with God.

King David, who is described as "a man after God's own heart," was constantly pouring out his questions, doubts, praises, and pain to God. When his soul was in turmoil, he was not afraid to tell God all about it. This messy soul directed itself to truth with a constant reminder of who God is. David listened to the Lord, recognising God was bigger than his problems. This must have been so precious to God. He often approaches our problems and pain with a piercing question. To Adam he asked, "Who told you that you were naked?" To Elijah he asked, "Why are you hiding in a cave?" To me He has said, "What does this breakup say about you Sarah?" These are the questions of a lover. Of someone caring enough to give you a voice.

Honest communication invites God into the space between where I am and where I want to be. This prayerful process directly places my heart in His hands. I become more open to hear and receive His guidance.

In this way, I will discover what is truly important.

Take a moment...

Q. What are the desires of your heart and how do you feel about them?

Q. How can you become more honest with God? Is there anything holding you back?

Q. Ask God to show you His perspective on your situation.

CHAPTER 18

THE ART OF WAITING

We don't like to wait. The very word reminds us of frustrating minutes and hours lost in airports, doctor's offices, traffic jams, and grocery lines. In these situations, we are paused until we can get to where we want to be. Whether we are sitting or standing, it feels like idleness and a waste of time. Waiting on the Lord is neither passive nor a waste of time. It may feel slow, but it is not like those other kinds of waiting. Those waits are just transitioning to some other place. When we are waiting on God, He is our destination, and we are actively pursuing with Him.

The Psalmist calls us to "Wait patiently for the Lord. Be brave and courageous" (Psalm 27:14 NLT). It takes a certain courage to wait on the Lord because it tests what we really believe about God. Do we try to control the dialogue or submit and listen for His voice? I have learned that waiting on the Lord requires active faith. When it comes to the promises of God, we can be tempted to 'help God' so that it happens sooner. We need to hold onto truth and allow God to do whatever He needs to do in His timing. There may be conditions we need to keep before other things occur. In the waiting, we hold God's hand and learn that He listens, cares, and show us things from His perspective. I love the prophet Isaiah's description of this process:

Yet those who wait for the LORD will gain new strength;
They will mount up with wings like eagles,
They will run and not get tired,
They will walk and not become weary.
Isaiah 40:31 (NASB)

Waiting on the Lord produces new strength and gives a heavenly perspective. Waiting prepares us for what is to come. It gives time for us to bring our questions and gain the answers and peace we seek.

Many people mentioned in the Bible had to wait. Joseph knew he was going to do something important one day and endured much suffering waiting for that to happen. David knew he was called to be King but had to wait for God's timing. Even Jesus waited for his 'time to come'. There is always something we will be waiting for. Our waiting produces mature faith, and ultimately a deep relationship with Jesus. Many mature Christians are still waiting on the Lord for promises to be fulfilled. God is not absent in the waiting. He is always moving. He uses seasons of waiting to develop the character in us necessary to steward the blessing. Managing an inheritance is hard work. We need more maturity, more discipline, more love to nurture the relationships, children, ministries, finances, and influence He wants to impart.

God is wise. Trust in His perfect timing.

Be careful how you apply the promises of God. I've see people longing for a marriage relationship give scriptures a distinctly personalised interpretation. Others hold onto a promise so furiously they make it into an idol. Others grow tired of waiting and find a way to make it happen that is not God's way.

So often the fulfilment of God's promise will look different than what we think. Israel waited thousands of years for a Messiah. They heard the prophets and read about the One who would come to free them from their oppression and establish a new kingdom. They knew the scriptures and trusted in the promise. When their Messiah Jesus finally came, they did not recognise Him. He was different than they expected. They were waiting for a great king and liberator. Jesus came humbly, leading people to love their enemies.

When God speaks to us about a particular situation, this 'word of the Lord' can be as simple as "trust me" or "wait." It can be a scripture God wants you to apply to your life. In Jeremiah 1:10-12, God asked Jeremiah to repeat back what He had heard and seen the Lord say. If the word you have from God is about a specific situation in your life, then the best way to interpret that word is through 'position' than 'prediction'. How are you preparing your heart to apply the word He brings?

A key to confirming a "word of the Lord" is allowing Him to bring it to pass in His way and in His timing. We each have free will. Therefore, we must continue to make decisions to remain in His will. The position of my heart is entirely up to me. God can reveal His will and I can refuse it. Others have free will too. If a "word of the Lord" you received involves another person, recognise that you all need to be in alignment with that word.

Is being happy essential?

People go into a romantic relationship for all kinds of reasons. Only you can know your 'why'. If you have the courage to be honest with yourself, God will expose your motives. It grieves me when I see friends who make ungodly compromises for the sake of a relationship. This can include differences in faith, compromising on personal values, or dating someone who has questionable character. I can never be the judge of someone's decisions so when I am concerned enough to ask why they are with this person I have noticed the answer usually falls back onto one comment.

"Yeah, but I'm happy." *Insert shoulder shrug.

Happiness is a fickle goal when it comes to relationship. Unlike joy, happiness is based on circumstances and in life circumstances constantly change. I never know what to say when being 'happy' is the reason for entering a relationship. Whilst I want my friends to be happy, I don't understand what it has to do with love. Happiness is a slippery servant. It is usually not there when we need it the most. What if the relationship becomes difficult and there is sorrow?

Our capacity to choose relationship is a God given privilege and responsibility. I choose to date someone because I like him and can see potential for something special to develop. I can be especially reassured in this decision if I see character in him. At some point, I may make another decision – to join my life with his in a marriage covenant. This commitment requires us to stay with our spouse even when their actions, choices, and words hurt my heart.

A desire to be 'happy' is not a bad thing; it just isn't supposed to be a value system or the goal of a relationship.

In any long-term romantic relationship, there will be times of joy and sadness. Our relational goal should be to love each other unconditionally.

CHAPTER 19

WHEN THE PRESSURE IS ON

When it comes to relationships and calling, one of the biggest mistakes you can make is to be driven by what Charles Hummel described as "the tyranny of the urgent."

The things we crave can create an internal pressure that builds until it feels urgent. That pressure leads to impulsive decisions, ones that give little thought to where those decisions will lead us tomorrow. Nobody wakes up and decides they will ruin their life in a day, but sometimes the big and little things we crave steal our eternal perspective and cause us to make foolish decisions. Consider this example from the story of brothers Jacob and Esau in Genesis 25:29-34 (NLT):

"One day when Jacob was cooking some stew, Esau arrived home from the wilderness exhausted and hungry. Esau said to Jacob, "I'm starved! Give me some of that red stew!" …

"All right," Jacob replied, "but trade me your rights as the firstborn son."

"Look, I'm dying of starvation!" said Esau. "What good is my birthright to me now?"

… So Esau swore an oath, thereby selling all his rights as the firstborn to his brother, Jacob.

Then Jacob gave Esau some bread and lentil stew. Esau ate the meal, then got up and left. He showed contempt for his rights as the firstborn."

The story begins with Esau in a vulnerable place. Maybe you have been there. You're emotionally and physically exhausted. You feel alone and misunderstood. Loneliness begins to crush your soul. You crave comfort. You want something, and you don't want to wait anymore. God is taking too long. What you need suddenly feels urgent.

Esau had a craving. He was impatient and sold his inheritance and his calling for a bowl of stew. A temporary hunger satisfied at the price of an eternal inheritance. Perhaps this doesn't seem so applicable to us. We would never plan to sell our inheritance so cheaply, but how many of us have gradually given in to a craving for love. We let go of something significant to grab a hold of something we think we desperately need in the moment. A moment moves on because it is temporary. We are left with regret – just as Esau was. We never graduate from being tested in our call.

As it happened to our forefathers Adam and Esau – and later to Jesus – at some point Satan will tempt us to trade our inheritance for something that fulfils only a temporary craving. God has an inheritance for you. Your 'call' first and foremost is a relationship with God. Your role, your status, your responsibilities will all change and look different throughout your life but the way you love God and others will always be important. When I look back at my life, I see a series of saying "yes" to Jesus. Sometimes it was a difficult yes and sometimes it was an excited yes. The call always comes, and it is my decision how I will respond. The call can look like a need, a concern, an opportunity, a problem, a relationship. I often think that we are called to steward the opportunities we are given. Our calling is not something we need to find. It is living inside of us. A relationship with God ignites it.

Yes, we will be tempted and distracted, but we needn't fall. Any desire that becomes the most urgent and important thing in our life is most likely an enemy of our souls.

What is your inheritance? What are the things God is directing you towards? What are the passions and the desires of your heart? What things and people has the Lord already entrusted you with? As children of God, we are heirs to the kingdom. God rewards with responsibility, and everyone who loves God will be given people and resources to steward. God wants to give us ownership because this is our calling - to partner with the Father. An inheritance has to do with responsibility, and if we are not willing to value what He has already given us we may lose it.

Recognise the urgent and let God show you what is important.

CHAPTER 20

BEYOND ROMANTIC LOVE

My aunt and uncle were the most incredible couple I have ever met. They were happily married for 52 years, and I learned so much about relationships from their example.

Their love story was like a movie. My uncle a notorious local bad boy (if street racing and smoking cigarettes makes you bad). My aunt was raised by strict but loving Christian parents. A random encounter brought them together and for him it was love at first sight. He pursued her, won over the parents, and married the girl of his dreams. They were best friends and lovers – and faithful followers of Jesus. My uncle adored my aunty and she respected him for who He was. They raised children, had grandchildren, and went though the ups and downs of life with incredible grace and kindness towards each other.

One time they lost almost everything they owned, including their beautiful family home, in an investment scandal. It was a life crisis that would have broken most people, but not them. They downsized, went back to work at retirement age, and continued to love each other. Their commitment to God and each other not only withstood the crisis but came out stronger.

After 50 years of marriage my uncle was diagnosed with a disease he never knew he had, In three weeks he was suddenly gone to be with Jesus. He spent his last moments on earth looking into his wife's eyes as she sat by his bedside. When my aunty became single again, her entire life changed. She learned to drive and to make the many day-to-day decisions that he once handled, or they had decided on together.

Their story challenges my own expectations of marriage. If we marry to avoid being alone what do we do when something we have no control over happens and ends the relationship? Amidst her grief, my aunty's faith in Jesus has held her steadfast.

A good marriage does not insure you from being 'alone' in life. So many couples have been forced apart over the years because of work, military service, illness or some crisis. The death of one you loved so well and so long must surely intensify the loneliness that results. After my uncle's passing, people would say to my aunt, "At least you had 52 years together." It is that very fact which makes a situation like hers more difficult. That's 52 years of life a certain way that suddenly changes without her permission.

Life brings many changes and death happens to all of us. The people we depend on may not be there for us in our darkest hour, and that is simply not fair. Change is the only constant in life and romantic love even at its best intent will have an earthly end. That's why the love relationship with Jesus is so important. His love is an everlasting one. His presence is with us always. Jesus fills our life with relationships so we can pour out His love to others in all seasons of life. My aunty now has a life filled with good relationships. She delights in her nephews, nieces, and a daughter and son who care about her. Her sister is her best friend. These relationships will not replace the person she has lost, but she is content and not alone.

Our calling to be in life-giving, eternal relationships goes far beyond romance and marriage.

PART SIX

LOVED

"Then, by constantly using your faith,
the life of Christ will be released deep inside you,
and the resting place of his love will become
the very source and root of your life."

Ephesians 3:17

CHAPTER 21

KNOWING YOUR TRUE IDENTITY

My father rode his motorbike for hours on a very cold morning to attend my graduation. As I was attaching my robe and hat, and preparing to take my seat, he surprised me with an unexpected gift. With near-frozen hands, he struggled to open a gift bag holding a small box. Inside was a gold ring with a stunning sapphire.

I immediately recognised the dark blue gemstone. Though I don't often wear jewellery, the ring is the most significant gift I ever received. Not because of what it was but because of what it represented. Dad had bought the sapphire for my mother during a visit to Jerusalem when I was a little girl. It was especially valuable because of the sacrifice my father had made to buy it at a time when things were financially difficult for our family.

Throughout my childhood, I would often join my mother as she was getting ready at her dresser and hold this sapphire in my tiny hands. It represented such love and sacrifice. At my graduation, Dad explained that he and Mum had agreed years ago to have the gem set in a ring and given to me. He presented it to me in the same box that had carried the sapphire home from Israel. Tears filled my eyes, not only because it was a beautiful gift, but because Dad remembered my childhood desire. The enormous effort he made to come to my graduation made this gift even more thoughtful and significant.

I always knew my parents loved me but now I was experiencing their love in a whole new dimension. It was a love that valued my heart. A love that noticed the details. The ring now sits in a special place in my room. Every time I take it out of the box, I know I am loved, and I feel grateful.

What does it look like to be loved? Is it having a boyfriend? A girlfriend? It is getting Valentine's Day flowers? Having many admirers pursue you or having thousands of followers on social media? What proof do we need to feel loved and okay about ourselves?

Not all of us know what it feels like to be loved. We may understand the concept and perhaps we have been told we are loved by others, but find it difficult to believe.

Love is not something we are informed about, it is something we experience. God has a divine love for you that is far too great to fully understand in one lifetime. How do we measure love? More importantly how do we feel loved?

I grew up in the church hearing that God loved me hundreds of times. Maybe you have too? The truth that God loves you is not supposed to be general information for the head but personally experienced in the heart. It's supernatural. Once you have encountered the love of God you will find true rest for your soul.

The love God gives is sweet and steadfast. It satisfies. It's deeply personal. From Genesis to Revelation the gospel story demonstrates a love that is everlasting. Many things in life may make us question if we are loved but God has given a strong reminder that will remain true even when we doubt. His name is Jesus. Just like the sapphire ring given by my father I can look to the cross and see a physical demonstration of God's commitment to me. But it doesn't just end there. The cross involves the resurrection, and a life of loving forever relationship in this life and in the age to come. The Holy Spirit further reveals the experience of God's love as our comforter, our helper, and advocate. This experience goes beyond informing us that we are loved. It gives that love a home in our hearts.

To be loved by God is our destiny. To love others as He does is our life calling. When I read 1 Corinthians 13, I realise that my love doesn't measure up to the standard Paul sets forth in this text. Unlike this God-defined love, my love has a limit. It gets tired. My love remembers wrongs. The agape love that God commands of us is not easy. It is a love that must depend on Jesus. We need Jesus to love like He loves. It's the gospel partnership of doing life with God that I begin to yield for the good of others. It is a decision to be kind, to be patient, to avoid keeping a record of wrongs. These choices often come at a time when I do not feel like being patient or kind. This is the way of God. He is stirring my heart to love like Him.

We may have romantic ideas about how it looks to be 'loving' in our Christian walk but it often looks like humility, repentance and forgiveness. Those words are not usually what I sign up for when considering a love story. This is the kingdom. To love involves keeping my heart soft when I want to make it tough, hard, and unaffected by others.

A person who knows they are loved can face the truth, be confronted, and take an honest look at their behaviour without questioning their value or worth. Regardless of past mistakes, wrong behaviour, or failures, God's love remains.

It was not achieved so it cannot be lost.

God has the love we need, and He does not withhold it. His love was never dependent on what we do. The love that comes from God provides inner strength for us to love others. God's love produces more love. It continually gives with abundant generosity.

The one who is loved has hope

I once spent a whole year trying to figure out what hope was. I always knew that hope was important. After all, it is listed alongside faith and love in the Bible. But how do we live a life of hope? Hope always seems like too much of a risk. Every life has its disappointments, and some are soul crushing. So how much should I hope for something to happen? Painful disappointment can make you never want to hope again.

I once heard someone say "hope hurts," and for many people it feels that way. Fear causes us to scale down hope to a level we can cope with. We play it safe. We don't lean into a beautiful anticipation of God's blessing. Instead, we decide that if what we cautiously hope for doesn't happen, we will still be okay.

Hope was easier to do when I was young and naive. As I got older, I settled for more 'realistic' expectations. I prayed weak prayers that weren't hopeful at all. God didn't abandon me in my weakness. He challenged my thinking, and taught me how to hope.

I read in the Psalms the call to "put your hope in God." According to the Bible 'hope' is good for the soul. So I began to search for how I could become better at hope. As I looked at the scriptures, I found a good definition of love in 1 Corinthians, and a clear concept of faith in Hebrews. But where were the instructions on hope? What does hope look like? Gradually the Lord began to teach me, and then one day I understood. I needed to redefine the very word. We don't hope in something, we hope in a someone.

Hope is actually spelled t-r-u-s-t.

To hope is to trust. If you replace the word 'hope' with 'trust' it still has the same meaning. We hope and we trust. I may not have known how to hope but I do know how to trust. Trust is easy when you know whom you are trusting. I fly all the time and pick airlines that I know will get me safely from A to B. When boarding a plane, I have never gone to the cockpit and asked the pilot to show me his or her aviation license and yet I am placing my life in their very hands.

We operate in such trust every day. We go to a cafe trusting they will have food and coffee, we bank online trusting that our money will go where we send it. We rock up to events and trust that there will be a performance from our favourite artist. There are occasions when things don't go as we had hoped, but we call those things into account. For believers, our hope in God rests upon His character and nature.

God is trustworthy. I can make bold requests, and I can share my desires openly to the Lord without fear. Real hope has taught me to approach God knowing that He hears my prayers and that His answer is for my best. I have learned that His "no" is as faithful as His "yes". If fear expects the worst, but love believes the best, then hope is anticipating what a good God will do. Trust in God will always produce hope. My hope is not dependent on whether what I am hoping for happens. It is dependent on who I am hoping in. I can trust God to make the best decisions for my life. People who are loved have hope. That's why biblical hope is so powerful.

They know the one who loves them will look after them. This perspective, which is so radically different from a secular worldview, keeps us anchored no matter how things turn out. It is why we have what Philippians 4:7 describes as peace "which transcends all understanding." There is a trustworthy anticipation of good in my life because I have placed my trust in a good God.

I am loved therefore I have hope.

Take a moment...

Q. Are there any areas of your life lacking hope?

Q. What would it mean to trust God in that specific area?

Q. How does your view of God impact your level of hope?

CHAPTER 22

LOVE AS FRIENDSHIP

An expensive blue box sits atop my dresser where it has been for years. It holds items that are most precious to me. If a burglar ever broke into my place, he likely would take it, assuming it was full of valuables. It is full of treasure, but not the bankable kind. It contains stacks of cards, letters, and photographs. Memories of times with my friends.

I've read each letter many times and stored cards so that each looks new. The photographs and ticket stubs are reminders of birthdays, camps, and events where we were together. During Covid-19 the whole world was discouraged from being together. Amid my own time of isolation, I rediscovered this box. I wrote letters, cards, and made phone calls to reconnect with the friends who were part of those sweet memories. I'm thankful we live in a world where connection is now accessible through technology, but nothing compares to the touch of human friendship.

As a young girl, I felt lonely and longed for deep friendships. I prayed for friends, and I believe the friends I have now are an answer to those prayers. Friends who laugh with me, confront me, and remind me of truth are a precious gift from God. A turning point in my life regarding friendships came through an unusual situation as a teenager. A girl from school called me and needed to talk. My favourite television show was on, and I didn't feel like hearing all about her breakup with a guy I never liked. I wanted to cut short the conversation, but something within me paid attention to the hurt in her voice. I shut off the television and listened. We talked for hours, and the next day at school we were best friends.

Friendships come to us in ways we are not expecting. Many of us miss out on these relational gifts from God because we're too busy with TV, video games, sports, shopping, and other interests to listen to others longing for friendship. But if we pay attention and value people, we will likely find a friend-in-the-making who will be loyal in our times of need.

In every healthy relationship there is laughter, tears, broken hearts, and new hearts. This is the stuff of friendship. Learning to care about a heart that is not your own. Cultivating friendship takes time and a little bit of routine. My friend and I cook pizza together on Monday nights. We have been doing it for years. Our routine is to talk, make food and share about our lives.

Another close friend moved to another state and later married. I determined that I would not let the distance and change in her relationship status cause us to drift apart. I purposed to call and visit regularly. When she got married, I felt as though I scored a brother. When they had children, I felt like an Aunty. I love spending time with their family. Somehow, we see each other every year and always share the big moments.

Friendships don't just happen. We make decisions that move towards them, we create the moments, we grab the opportunities, and we choose how we spend our time.

I am grateful to have a home church that is big on friendships. My church is passionate about missions, families, and youth ministry - the same things as me. I love going to church. It took me a long time to find a church that felt like home. I love the way we worship, I love the teaching, but mostly I love the people I meet and get to start friendships with. Long after the church service has ended, we are still talking. I look at the people I go to church with; their personality, careers, and it occurs to me that we would never have crossed paths unless it had been at church. I love the diversity. I love the relationships. This is the kingdom. This is what God desires for his people. Coming together.

It is so good to avoid limiting your friendships to people who are like you or are your own age. I have friends who are 18 and friends who are in their 70s. I want friends who are both married and unmarried. I don't want to assess my connection with others by their relationship status. If we only relate with people who are like us we miss out on so much! I am particularly grateful for my older friends. Men and women who society would call elderly are experts at things I am still trying to figure out. Best of all, they have the time for long conversations. I appreciate this and enjoy their wisdom and perspective. Imagine if we stepped outside of our cultural frameworks and into a kingdom model that crosses barriers of age and social status.

There is a natural human tendency to seek friendship with people who are like us. Similar in age, ethnicity, marital status, with or without children, by religion or denomination, education level, social status, political views, etc. The church as Jesus intended it isn't like that.

It aims to form people of diverse backgrounds into one body, united in their love and devotion to him. The Kingdom of God only grows as people take seriously Christ's Great Commission call to "go and make disciples of all nations." Though you may never venture to another country, all of us who follow Jesus must heed his call to go out and build discipling relationships with people who are different from us.

I believe much of the loneliness in the world is self-imposed because people, even Christians, won't venture beyond their own social groupings or invest the time needed to form deep friendships. Much of the racial strife today is for the same reason. It's easier to make "us and them" judgments when you have no friends within a particular group. So let's break that pattern. God delights in loving human relationships. He delights in the peoples and cultures he has made. One day we all will be joined for eternity (Rev. 7:9). For now, we can bring Heaven here on earth and begin living like God intends for us to live. The more years I live the more I value my friendships and I have learned that there is always someone who needs a friend. I want to go deep with people and talk about their story.

As I reach out to get to know others my heart grows a little more, and this is beautiful.

CHAPTER 23

FREE TO LOVE

The Webster Dictionary defines courage as "the ability to do something afraid." How do we gain this ability?

By faith.

What we believe about God and his faithfulness will always impact the way we love. God has been calling His people to courage for thousands of years. We need courage to live for God and to love others. Courage comes not just by believing God is who He says He is, but by trusting what he is doing in our lives. It is His very presence that gives you the ability to step out when you're afraid.

The relational issues presented in this book may seem daunting. But by faith, God will help you overcome them all. Remember, faith is based on the nature and character of God. He has said, "Be strong and courageous ... for the Lord your God will be with you wherever you go" (Joshua 1:9). So take courage to face your fears concerning relationships.

What is your deepest fear?

To be alone? Unloved? Most fears hide a lie that we have come to believe is true. These lies sound like truth because they can contain a few facts. They often point out our past failures, weaknesses, and sins. They want us to conclude God doesn't truly love us, that we are beyond help, and that we are worthless. Satan presses us to make important decisions about our identity based on those lies, and fear promotes this.

Jesus came to expose and help you overcome all such lies. He says, "I am the Way, the Truth, and the Life." I'm still amazed that we can have a personal relationship with truth. Jesus is truth, and when we embrace Him as Lord, He shines the light of truth into our lives. He exposes lies we didn't even know we were believing. Truth sets us free from fear and teaches us to love.

I love the story of Jesus and the woman at the well (John 4). It is such a strong illustration of how the truth works through relationship. Jesus talks with someone nobody else wanted to spend time with. His act of love opened her heart to the truth. Jesus didn't give her relationship advice. He gave her living water. She was thirsty for forgiveness and hope, a thirst that was not going to be met by relationships with more men. Her thirst was met through the redeeming love of Jesus.

The more I learn about God's nature and character, the more I realise what freedom we have to approach our loving Father. We can make bold requests. I can ask as a daughter, and you can ask as a son. I can ask for anything and trust that His "no" is as faithful as His "yes." That is real faith. Trusting God's character even when He doesn't do what you think He should be doing. God is always good, always holy, always faithful. These attributes do not depend on the outcomes of my prayers.

The result of trusting God is peace, even when confronting our biggest fears. Jesus tells us not to allow our hearts to be troubled (John 14:27). The rest He promises is born from active faith, from courageously staking our future on Him.

Many people are still trying to achieve love as though it is a goal. Because they make it a goal, their hearts and minds are constantly working for it. They become like a cat chasing its tail. We are not meant to work for something that has already been freely given. The way to obtain this love is to accept who God says you are and receive His love. God Himself wants to fulfil our deepest need for love. How mind-blowing it is that the God of the universe would extend His heart for relationship with us. He desires you. He desires me. He is the good shepherd who cares about His sheep. When we embrace the love of God, we learn to love others in the way that is only possible through God.

In this book, I have promoted the great value of Christian friendship. We all need friendship and a strong sense of belonging. But our life foundation needs to be anchored to something way more consistent than friendship. Even the deepest friendships can change due changes of location, changes of relationship status, and the tides and seasons of life. Our sense of identity and purpose must be built on Christ; the only solid rock. You belong to the Lord. He will never leave you. Your confidence in His love will give you the courage to face any life challenge.

A love like no other

A person who knows they are loved will not try to earn love. They will not need to gain a relationship status to measure their significance, value or worth. They do not live to achieve, perform, or impress others. They have an honoured place in the Kingdom of God. What more could they hope to gain?

Jesus described the Kingdom in many ways. Ultimately, the kingdom is about us living in right relationship with God and others. What is called The Great Commandment affirms that. We are commanded and empowered to love God "with all our heart, mind, soul, and strength" and to form loving relationships with others.

Knowing you are loved will change your perspective. It will motivate you to reach out and welcome others into your heart and home. Loved people take action. Love gives. To give love empowers. To demand love leaves us wanting. I find that the more I give love, the more I am blessed to receive it. I think this is the way love is supposed to work out in our lives. I can love freely and the more I give away, the more abundance I receive in the outworking of love.

A child of God cultivates relationships that love deeply. We befriend both married and unmarried people because it is 'good' and 'godly' for humans to be in relationship. We form relationships across generations, cultures, and social class. Why? Because this is what

Jesus said to do. Because we will be richer in Kingdom life when we do.

I hope that in reading this book you have learned with certainty that your value is not dependent on your relationship status. Our need for love and value will never be fulfilled in a relationship status. No title before your name will assure you of life-long love. Only God can assure you of that. He has already confirmed it by giving you the gift of Jesus. Our deepest need can only be met in Him. He is truth, and all strong relationships are built on Truth. Truth teaches us to love and extends our hearts beyond what they looked like yesterday.

You may be one who feels abandoned, rejected, and unable to relate to others in the way you desire. How the Lord must long to show you how valued you are and welcome you into His eternal family! Perhaps you have a fear of facing the truth in case you don't like what you find. If that is you, Jesus will meet you in that lonely space. He is the God who pursues and makes a way for you to love like He loves. To give you a life full of relationships!

I am forever grateful for the relationships He has given me. I can never repay all those people who have helped me on my life journey, but I can honour them by helping others. I can teach others to trust in God, to hope in God, and to anchor their relationships in Him. There is something strong and beautiful about hope. Hope moves the soul into a steady position of high trust.

If you desire marriage, anchor your hope in Jesus. He is the author and perfecter of our faith (Hebrews 12:2). Marriage is a wonderful relationship covenant. It is a good thing to desire, but it is not a safeguard against loneliness. It is also not the only option to a life filled with relationship. Married or unmarried we are all called to cultivate relationships throughout our lifetime. Married or unmarried we all need to keep our hearts soft and open. Married or unmarried you will need vision for your life that wakes you up in the morning excited to gain more of God's heart for others. Living this way through all the uncertainties of life is only possible when you know how much God deeply loves and cares for you. He is a father who calls you by name. The God who restores hope and dignity to all who receive Him.

The truth is, you are loved.

How will you respond to His love? Through the Holy Spirit, you are capable of experiencing a forever love that is beyond your wildest imagination in this life and the life to come.

ACKNOWLEDGEMENTS

This book has been a deeply personal process with an incredible team of talented individuals who helped make it happen.

Caitlin Fisher was my first reader. She tackled the messy first draft, suggesting edits and encouraging me to turn this project into a book.

It would not have been possible without my incredible editor Scott Tompkins. I knew this book was meant to be when God provided such a veteran editor. Scott spent countless hours going over the manuscript (and condensing my very long paragraphs). Scott's articulate insight and honest, thoughtful feedback refined this book's message into what you have in your hands today. Thank you so much, Scott!

Grace - you are so talented. Your creativity always produces the goods!

Several proofreaders generously gave their time to review and challenge my ideas, causing me to go deeper into my beliefs. Lael Piteau, you are one of my dearest friends. Thank you. Sam Giunta your feedback was transformational in helping me articulate my view of calling. The wonderful Kris Skinner championed this book and gave her time whilst operating in a senior leadership position. Shout out to Charis Jackson who flicked through the book during her London lockdown, sending a thumbs up. Thanks to Chris Ryburn for revising my chapter summaries. And to Dean Sherman - your encouragement in the early days was life-giving. Appreciate you!

Lastly, I want to acknowledge my parents Brian and Raylee, who introduced their daughter to Jesus and gave her a Bible as a child. This caused me to think eternally when it came to relationships.

Forever grateful. xo